PLACE IN RETURN BOX to remove this checkout ˙ ‑ord.
TO AVOID FINES return on or before date due.

˙ ꞓ ‾ ˙TE DU‾

TRENDS IN RURAL POVERTY

TRENDS IN RURAL POVERTY

BY

G. BHASKAR

RBSA PUBLISHERS
S.M.S. Highway, Jaipur
(India)

Published by

DEEPAK PARNAMI
RBSA Publishers, S.M.S. Highway,
Jaipur - 302 003 (India)

G. BHASKAR

1994

ISBN 81-85813-13-2

Computerised/typesetting by:
Amit Bhargava
B - 206, Bapu Nagar,
Jaipur - 302 015

Printed at
Harihar Printers, Jaipur

ACKNOWLEDGEMENTS

I am greatly indebted to Dr. A. Sadanandam, Reader in Economics, Kakatiya University, under whose supervision this work is carried out. He has been kind enough to spare his valuable time for guidence, computerisation of data and analysis of the results.

It has been a great pleasure and privilege to have worked under him. But without his valuable guidance, personal affection and encouragement, this work would not have been completed.

I express my deep sense of gratitude to Dr. N. Linga Murth, Head, Department of Economics, Kakatiya University, for his kind advice and encouragement. I am greatful to Prof. C. Siva Rama Krishna Rao, Dr. B. Shyamala Devi, Reader, G. Rajaiah, Reader, and Dr. K. Venkat Narayana, Lecturer, for their invaluable suggestions and co-operation.

I am beholden to Prof. V.V. Reddy, Regional Engineering College, Warangal, who is the guiding force to undertake this study.

I am very much indebted to my dearest friend, Sri M. Yadagira Charyulu, Lecturer in Economics, Sathupally, without whose help, I would not have completed this streneous job. It is my duty to mention here, my friend Dr. A. Vinayak Reddy, who has extended his helping hand at every stage of my work. I am also thankful to Dr. T. Jogaiah, Reader in Commerce, Kakatiya University, for his whole hearted support.

I am greatful to the Vice-Chancellor, the Registrar and Dean, Social Sciences Faculty, for enabling me to submit my Thesis prior to the stipulated time.

I may be at fault, if I do not mention the name of Dr. R.Laxmipathi, Chief Planning Officer, Warangal, who has helped me in obtaining the relevant data. I am also thankful to the Respondents of my study area, who have extended their co- operation during the field study.

It is my bounden duty to express my thanks to Smt. Rama Sadanandam, Miss Hema and Sambaiah for their skillful task of computerised typing.

Finally, I would like to express my gratitude to my close associates Sri K. Samba Murthy, Sri G. Vishwanadham, Sri V. Venkateshwar Rao, V. Yagneshwar and S. Madusudhana Chary.

G.BHASKAR

CONTENTS

CONTENTS

1

POVERTY: A HISTORICAL PERSPECTIVE

A study of poverty of the nations has a greater relevance today even after so many measures have been taken by various governments and International organisations to eradicate the global poverty because mass poverty exists in vast areas of Asia, Africa and Latin American countries. Even the developed countries have some pockets of mass poverty. However, the problem is acute in the developing countries. The poverty has its origin in the feudalistic relations of production. The collective degradation of hundreds of millions of human beings with such mass poverty is a shocking commentary on the whole texture of human existence as well as the true content of apparent human values in the third world, or perhaps in the world as a whole. [1]

GENESIS OF POVERTY: SOME APPROACHES

There are numbers of contending views regarding the genesis of poverty. If it is believed that the word poverty is a result of too many people and too few goods, then the basic strategy must be to reduce the growth of population and increase the supply of goods. If we believe that over time the laws of supply and demand will establish an optimal equilibrium in the National and Inter national context, then we must be careful not to interfere with the operation of those laws. If the fundamental cause of world poverty is the ability of the privileged to protect and extend their privileges, then there is a need to bring out the changes in the existing structure as a precondition of the eradication of the global poverty. There are various schools of thought taking different approaches in analysing the nature of the poverty. The classicals and neo-classicals regard market mechanism as a remedial measures to all the sins of the economy, but the notion proved to be incorrect with the advent of Keynesian revolution. The structuralists, on the other hand, lay emphasis on market flies in the face of the fact that the most cursory examination of any developing country reveals the imperfection of the market mechanism. Interest groups institutions and structures of all sorts- political, administration, legal, tenurial and industrial- combined to ensure that markets work imperfectly. Markets are manipulated, and influenced to work in ways that don't conflict with the perceived interests of those in power.[2] This would be a basis for neo-marxist analysis. The neo-marxist approach starts from an analysis of distribution of political power and seeks to explain it in terms of the distribution of the ownership of productive assets.[3] There is another view that poverty, and impoverishment is the result of a casual process of which enrichment is a major but not exclusive component. Three different processes of enrichment and impoverishment can be identified. The process of selection, which determines socio- economic status; the intra-group competitions, which determines the individuals who acquired control over the resources within the group; and inter group competition, which determines how resources are divided between groups with obviously different interests. We may also emphasize here that the eternal existence of poverty is due to the fact that motivations and attitudes of the interest groups are working against the poor. Though their size, political lever age, organisation and inter-relationship obviously vary from country to country, they include the political elite, the bureaucratic elite, the owners of businesses, large farmers (land lords) etc. They manipulate the process of selection in order to limit the risk of downward mobility for themselves and to ensure that the structures that benefit them, are adequately served with appropriately trained manpower.[4]

Mass poverty is a situation where a large percentage of population suffers from a chronic shortage of food and other basic needs like clothing, housing, medical, and educational facilities and hence are victims of ill-health, disease, sheer animal hunger, reduced longevity and ignorance which is an obvious phenomenon in any third world country. The concentration of mass poverty in the developing countries and of economic affluence in the developed countries has, however, come into existence only during the last two centuries or so. In ancient times the developed countries had no civilization comparable to that of the Indus Valley, Nile Valley, Yangtse Valley or to the Maya and Inca Civilizations of the South. But the industrial revolution transformed the techno-economic infrastructure of Europe and it paved for the acceleration of economic development, which was not spread to the developing countries for the first time in the history. After that, industrial nations even completed what is called the second industrial revolution and entered into the threshold of third stage. On the other hand the developing countries are labouring in the first phase of the kind of industrial revolution. This major divergence in the level of techno-economic progress in the two hemispheres is generally regarded as the prime cause for the economic advancement of developed nations and the relative economic backwardness of developing countries, of which mass poverty is the predominant characteristic. It should be noted here in this connection that the contemporary developed countries also experienced mass poverty in the earlier stages of their modern economic development. England started experiencing the problem of large scale poverty in the Tudo period which was further intensified by the growing unemployment in the first phase of the industrial revolution during the seventeenth and eighteenth centuries. The rest of the Western Europe also experienced the same. In the U.S.A., several million African slaves, Red Indians paid the price of modern economic development, although virtually unlimited land and natural resources were available for the purpose. Even in Japan mass poverty not only existed during the Tokugawa era but even after the Meiji restoration.[5] But mass poverty in these countries was progressively eradicated through rapid economic development relatively over a long period of time in the capitalistic countries than the Soviet Union.

The tragedy of contemporary mass poverty in the South is much more staggering in its dimensions than that of developed countries in their entire history of economic development, that the pace of economic development in the developing nations is much slower than that of developed countries in the corresponding historical phase of its industrialisation. The historical development of capitalism and its highest stage of imperialism and the wanton victimisation of the developing countries by the developed one are essential and unavoidable historical data in the aetiology of poverty in general and large scale poverty in the third world in particular.

The situations that are now prevailing in the third world countries are the cumulative result of rapid evolution of European imperialism into North-Western neo-imperialism, historically evolved, structural factors responsible for engendering mass poverty among the majority of the world's population. The structures of these national societies are also under the influence of imperialism and neo-imperialism. Therefore, mass poverty in the developing countries is not simply a matter of a micro-economic theory or a macro-economic theory of savings, investments in a low level equilibrium, or even a macro-dynamic theory of economic growth involving econometric models of the factors and conditions of economic growth, without any reference to historical structures.[6]

On the basis of per capita income, Prof. Siman Kuznet classified India and the South-East and middle-east countries as under developed, where per capita national income was below 100 U.S. dollars.[7] It is hardly necessary to stress that a per capita income of 100 U.S. dollars is hardly sufficient to provide a decent level of living. Yet many under-developed countries are helplessly caught in a low level equilibrium trap and exposed themselves to a secular trend of low levels of income.[8] Ragnar Nurkse improvised the concept of vicious circle of poverty, he wrote "the concept implies of course a circular constellation of forces tening to act and react upon one another in such a way as to keep a poor country in a state of poverty".[9] Because of low per-capita income the level of saving and investment would be low, and with low level of investment poor worker productivity, and therefore, per capita income would also remain low.[10]

Before going into the clutches of British colonial rule, India had its prestigious saga with a high quality methods of production and commercial organisations. It had a prominent places in international market. India had manufactured and exported the finest muslins and other luxurious fabrics and articles at the time when the ancestors of the British were living extremely primitive life.[11] India's abilities for the use of steam power and to mechanise her traditional trades and crafts was also great indeed in view of her rich endowment of natural resources. Thus, in the words of D.H. Buchanan, here (India) was a country with all the crude elements upon which manufacturing depends with abundant supplies of raw cotton, raw jute, coal, high grade iron ore, with a hoard of gold and silver, second perhaps to no other country in the world with an excellent market within her own borders and near hand.[12]

Thus, any explanation of India's under-development in terms of poor natural resources endowment, absence of indigenous talents, socio cultural factors, or over population etc., doesn't correspond with facts.[13]

Marx rightly explained India's under development and wide spread poverty in terms of the impact of British rule. He envisaged for England a double mission in India, one destructive, the other regenerating- the annihilation of the old Asiatic in India.[14] In the earlier period the initial steps of destruction were completed first by the East India Company's policy of direct plunder and subjugation of India. This policy resulted in the transportation of the treasures from India to England and the neglect of irrigation and public works led to the decline of agriculture and the introduction of British land system and the criminal courts which finally established private property rights in land and other means of production, and finally the prohibition of or imposition of heavy duties on the import of Indian manufactures first into England and later in Europe, had resulted in the destruction of India's traditional crafts and trade.[15]

During the 19th century came the invasion of English industrial manufactures, and with this the pre-capatalist Indian economic structure was totally wrecked. In the words of Marx "British steam and science uprooted the whole surface of Hindostan, the Union between agriculture and manufacturing".[16] The adverse effects of Britain's cotton machinery on Indian weavers was put-forth by Governor-General's report of 1834-35, in the following: "the misery hardly finds a parallel in the history of commerce, the bones of the cotton weavers are bleaching the plains of India.[17]

To sum up the results of British colonial rule in India in the words of Baran, "the British administration of India systematically destroyed all the fibers and foundations of Indian society. Its land and taxation policy ruined India's village economy and substituted for it the parasitic land owner and money lender". Its commercial policy destroyed the artisan and created the slums of Indian cities filled with millions of starving and diseased paupers. Its economic policy broke down whatever beginnings there were of an indigenous industrial development and promoted the proliferation of speculators petty businessmen, agents and sharks of all descriptions eking out a sterile and precarious livelihood In the masses of a decaying society.[18]

Jawahar Lal Nehru had observed that the poorest regions of Colonial India were the regions longest of all under the yoke of British Colonialists. Naoroji had traced the mass poverty in India to the British colonial rule which drained out enormous amounts of wealth through unequal trade, interest and dividends, salaries and pensions besides, the colonial administration extracted larger amounts of revenues from native citizens through arbitrary taxation in order to maintain a repressive colonial administration.[19] The main cause of India's poverty, according to Dadabi was the enormous 'drain' of the produce of the country to England 'chiefly arising from the political position it held over India'. The drain was in the form of excess of exports over imports between 1835 and 1872, this excess amounted to $ 500,000,000 which England kept back as its benefit.[20] Empirical estimates by the contemporary authors, Sir Percival Griffiths has estimated the 'tribute' (drain) from India between 1750 and 1800 at dollars 100 to 150 millions in money of that period also strengthened the contention of Dadabai Naoroji.[21] While William Digby estimated it for the period between Plassey and Water Loo (1757 to 1815) at * 18 million a year or a total of about * 1000 million.[22] Holden estimated that during the decade 1783-93, the amount transferred unrequited from India to Britain was something under *2 million.[23] Robert Mont Gomrey Martin testified before a British Parliamentary Committee in 1840 that estimating the unrequited sums of money drawn from British India during the preceding 30 years at * 3 million per annum.[24] A typical example of the devastation caused to the colonial economies by such thickly veiled plunder in the name of trade was the destruction of the economy of Bengal and the Indo-Gangetic plain by the East India Company. The natural wealth and cash crops of the region were more or less physically looted and shipped out to England. [25] The indigenous industries disappeared, partly due to the outright destruction by the British and partly due to competition from imported manufactures, throwing millions of people out of employment. One immediate result of the first phase of the plunder, has both British and Indian historians agreed was the Bengal famine of the 1770's which wiped out nearly half the population of the province. A second consequence of great economic significance was the reverse migration of people from towns to the villages ushering in a process of economic retrogration.

The main consequence of India's integration with the British rule was that the historical process of evolution from a pre-industrial economy to a developed industrial economy was interrupted. Consequently the transformation of pre-capatalist agrarian relations couldn't take place in India in the way it did in the independent countries of the Western Europe. Her land tenures, on the other hand, were adopted and modified to suit the economic and political requirements of the British economy.[26] In order to reorganise agrarian structure of India, the Britishers established two types of land systems in the country, viz. the Zamindari and Ryothwari. Under the Zamindari tenure the rights of property in land were conferred on the native tax gatherers who had never taken any interest in actual cultivation. As a result millions of persons who had been propritor-cultivators for a long were reduced to the position of tenants-at-will on their own lands. Under Ryothwari system also heavy revenue assessments led to the pauperisation of the cultivator and to the alienation from his own land. During the whole course of the 19th century, the pre-capitalist forms of exploitation had robbed the agriculturists of the major part of the fruits of their labour.[27] The land- lord tenant nexus was further strengthened by the pressure generated by the increasing penetration of colonial trade into agricultural produce. The growth of trade in raw materials and the inundation of the market with Britain's machine made goods weakened the very basic foundations of village self-sufficiency by disrupting the indigeneous handi-crafts in both the towns and the villages. The same process had accelerated the penetration of commodity-money relations in the country. This created certain conditions for the speedy development of capitalistic production which destructed self-sufficiency of villages and for a large number of peasants and rural artisans created a labour market. Actually, the capitalist system of production which was accelerated, by British rule, enabled them to subordinate India's agricultural production according to their requirements. Further, the labour market created as a result of large scale alienation of peasants and artisans led only to the pauperisation of the masses without absorbing them in modern industry as in the Western capitalist countries.[28]

Thus, the development of a commodity economy along the capitalist lines under the foreign rule, instead of creating circumstances for the growth of agriculture on modern methods served to strengthen the oppressive landlordism by means of which economic surplus from the agricultural sector was extracted by a conglomeration of rentiers, merchants and usurers. The utilisation of surplus for conspious consumption and as usurious capital prevented productive investment in agriculture which caused further backwardness of agriculture.[29]

INDIAN RURAL AGRARIAN SCENE ON THE EVE OF INDEPENDENCE

At the stroke of independence the agrarian structure was plagued and had a socio-economic set up in which parasitism flourished, land concentration in the hands of rural rich continued to grow, and land-lessness and land hunger of the peasants mounted at an ever increasing pace. Evictions and insecurity of tenants and rock-renting became a general phenomenon and the cultivators were ground down by a colossal burden of indebtedness.[30] Rentals continued to increase throughout the 20th century and in some reported cases the rents out stripped the agricultural prices, and reached the level of three quarter of gross produce. Besides this, illegal levies imposed on tenants and share- croppers reinforced their conditions of servitude. Ever increasing absentee landlordism on the one hand and the parasitical dependence of landless masses on big semi-feudal land owners on the other existed in the same time in all parts of the country. Thus, what emerged from the British impact was pattern of structural change without economic growth; no capitalist enterprise based on modernisation of the mode of production and the consequent enlargement of the economic surplus in the hands of dynamic producers but a semi-feudal structure based on ruthless extraction of surplus by the parasitical trinity of landlords-money lenders-traders from peasant producers attached to primitive methods of production. A highly skewed land distribution, wide spread share-tenancy, excess dependence on agriculture and interlocked factor markets are some of the more aggressive features of existing agrarian production relations that are supposed to inhibit not only the transition to a more progressive agriculture, but block even the trickle-down of benefits to the rural poor of whatever little increase in farm production occurs in such a socio-economic mile.[31]

Agrarian structure of a country, as it well known, is the historically evolved compound outcome of the laws, customs, institutions, rural power configurations and a host of other factors that shape the relations of production and govern the distribution of agricultural net product among various groups regions, classes involved in and dependent on agriculture. In the contemporary literature one finds two mechanisms through which regressive feature of the agrarian structure manifest and keep the masses of the rural in perpetual poverty. One of these is supposed to operate by retarding agricultural development and lowering the amount of agricultural net product available for distribution, and the other operates by inequitably distributing this net product among rural classes that share and subsist on it. For convenience of expression, the first can be called

Agricultural Development Channel and the second Direct Distributional Channel. The regressive features of the agrarian structure result in lowering the agricultural net product itself via mechanisms like low output per acre on big farms; higher proportion of uncultivated land on big farms and disincentives in the adoption of new technology created by share tenancy and sizable peasants with un-economic holdings and interlocked factor markets. The direct distributional effect on the agrarian structure can also operate though the number of ways, being according to its position in the matrix of production relations. Given the size of agricultural net product, the incidence of poverty among the self-employed cultivating house-holds depends mainly on the degree of inequality in its distribution and that is directly determined by the degree of inequality in the distribution of land they operate. Poverty among share-croppers is mainly due to excessive surplus extraction by land-lords enabled by their near monopoly resulting from high degree of land concentration. Similarly, segmentation of the rural labour markets, the glut of wage-labourers in the country-side and their weak bargaining power resulting from land-lessness and low political awareness and mobilisation are believed to manifest in low wage rates, irregular employment and mass poverty among these rural proletarians. [31A]

The village artisans and craftsmen including blacksmiths cobblers, potters, weavers, fishermen, carpenters though self-employed, this class generally shares the poverty of the lower economic strata of the peasantry, and in the socio-economic structure of the country is unable to rise above the poverty line. Lacking in capital and modern technology, operating on a very low scale of production and catering to a very limited market, this class represents more of a legacy of the past than of a promise for the future and persists on a level of bare subsistence and absolute poverty mainly on account of the relative economic stagnation and socio-economic inertia. These sections constitute the over whelming majority of the rural poor and generally live below the poverty line in the rural sector. Poverty, for instance is no abstract draw-back of the economy; it is the concrete fact that all over the country still, there are men, women and children who do not have enough food to eat. It is the problem of the thousands of villagers in the dry regions of Andhra Pradesh, Tamilnadu, Rajasthan, Orissa, Madhya Pradesh and Bihar who do not have drinking water within their reach. It is a fact that the farmers do not have a land of their own to cultivate and cannot find enough work in other's farms. It is the problem of the ongoing millions of urban as well as rural who do not have a roof over their heads. Unsuccessful and poor farmers are not confined to the ecologically difficult areas only, in the less difficult areas also, poverty may result from an unwillingness or inability to adopt new technology or having adopted it, to maintain it. Most relevant to our concerned are those who wish to adopt the new technology but find that, they are denied access to adequate land, inputs and adequate markets. It can be observed that the enrichment of some sections of the rural community has been at the cost of the absolute or relative impoverishment of those who have been excluded from access to land.

The deprivation of access to the inputs or markets or land force the poor farmers to seek alternative ways of making a living. At worst the poor farmer may be driven off the land altogether and become a landless labourer. At best he will take casual work during off-season to earn a little extra cash. Between these two extremes lies another group, who may sell their only salable asset-labour. The most common situation is for one or more of the adult males to migrate in search of work, leaving the women and children, with perhaps some adult males, to secure at least, a subsistence from the land.

Majority of the rural masses in India hardly make a living wage, they do not have any surplus. They are even deprived of the basic necessities like health and education. As the per capita income of these sections is very low, they are not even at remote access to these developments. Privatisation of medical facilities further accentuated the problems of rural poor. They have to go to far off places for the medical aid. The education system is not yet related to the living conditions, aspirations and environment of the rural masses. The schools and colleges do not inculcate among the students to respect the dignity of labour, without which no nation can rise out of its poverty.

Malnutrition and under nourishment, infant mortality which are the resultant health hazards of acute poverty hinder the sound development of society and have an adverse effect economic productivity. The rural structure which is in the midst of the host of problems like socio-economic dualism, over dependence on agriculture, poor health and education, mass poverty is not only due to the colonial rule but also the confidence-mechanism [32] (con-mech) which is working in all walks of our society. The 'confidence-mechanism' assures the deprived, destitute sections who are ruthlessly exploited, that they will have a chance to get the benefits from the existing production relations. But in practice they won't have a 'say' in on-going system. The men behind this con-mech generously give concessions and introduce reforms in the name of upliftment of poor in such a way, where there won't be any interruption to the previlages that they are enjoying in the existing society.

NOTES & REFERENCES:

1. Bandopadhyaya.J   :   The poverty of Nations, (A global perspective of mass poverty in the third world) Allied Publishers, Pvt.Ltd. Ahmedabad. 1987. P.3.

2. Charles Elloitt   :   Patterns of the poverty in the third world, Praeger Publishers, New-York, 1975. P.2.

3. William G   :   For a particularly fine summery of Neo-Marxism that does justice to its diversity as well as its intelectual unity, see Aidan Foster-Carter, "Neo-Marxist approaches to Development and Under development", in sociology and development, eds, Ed.de Kadl and G.William (London : Tavistock 1974.pp.67 to 108).

4. Charless Elliott   :   Op.cit. p.10.

5. Bandopadhyaya J   :   Op.cit. p.3.

6. Bandopadhyaya J   :   Op.cit. p.6.

7.   :   Post-War economic growth, Massachusetts, 1964, p.29 also see Patel.S.J. "The economic distance between nation, its origin, measurement and outlook", the Economic Journal, March, 1964.

8. Nelson R.R   :   A theory of low level of equilibrium trap in under development economies, The American Economic Review. Vol.46 No. 5 1956.

9. Nurkse R   :   Problem of capital formation in under developed countries, Oxford 1953 p.4.

10. Nurkse R   :   Ibid and also see Madam B.K. (ed), Economic problem of U.D.C. in Asia, New Delhi 1954.

11.   :   Economic development of India (London), p.5.

12.   :   The Development of capitalist enterprize in India, New-York, 1934, p.(450).

13. Dutt R.P   :   India today, Calcutta 1979 p.45.

14. Marx Engles   :   The future results of British rule in India on cononialism, Moscow 1978 p.82.

15.   :   The East India Company, its history and results, Mascow, 1978.pp.45 to 54. also see R.P.Dutt, India today, Calcutta 1979 p.88.

16. Marx Engles   :   The British rule in India op.cit.p.38,39.

17. Marx, A.K   :   Capital, Vol. I, Mascow 1954, p.432.

18. Barun A Paul   :   The political economy of growth, New-Delhi 1958 p. 282 to 283.

19. Naoroji Dadabhai : Poverty of India, Winck Worth Foulgar and Co. The Aldine Press London 1888 p.34.

20. : Ibid

21. Sir Percival Griffiths : The British impact in India, Macdonald, London 1952 p.374, p. 375.

22. William Digby : Prosperous British India: A revelation from official records, T.Fister Unwin, London 1901 p. 33.

23. Holden Furber : John company at work, Harward University Press 1948, cited in Johns' Strachey, the end of Empire, Victor Gollancz, London 1954, p. 63.

24. Robert Mart : The history, antiquities, topography and statistical of Eastern India, W.H. Allen, London 1838 Vol.1 Introduction.

25. Naoroji Dadabhai : op. cit. p. 141.

26. Ramesh Dutt : op.cit Vol. 1 p.292 also Sumit Sarkar, Modern India 1885- 1947, Macmillian Delhi 1983 pp. 24 to 28.

27. Joshi P.C : Land Reforms in India, A.R. Desai (ed): Rural sociology, Popular Prakashan, 1969 p. 444.

28. Joshi P.C : op. cit 445.

29. : Ibid p. 446.

30.   :   Ibid p. 448.

31. Sisodia O.P   :   Land reforms for social change,
                                       Kurukshetra, Vol. XXXVIII No. 3
                                       December 1989, p. 16,17. Thinkers
                                       Library. The Technical Publishing
                                       House, Allahabad 1987, p. 30.

32. Charles Elliott   :   Charles Elliott coined the concept of
                                       confidence-mechanism (con- mech) in
                                       his poineer work entitled 'Patterns of
                                       Poverty' in the third world.

2

CONCEPT OF POVERTY: SOME METHODOLOGICAL ISSUES IN INDIAN CONTEXT

Poverty can be defined as a social phenomenon in which a section of the society is unable to fulfill even its basic necessities of life.[1] C.T. Kurien defined poverty as the socio-economic phenomenon whereby the resources available to a society are used to satisfy the wants of the few while many do not have even their basic needs met.[2] Poverty is generally manifested in terms of low incomes, inadequate housing, poor health, limited or no education, high infant mortality, low life and work expectancy, and in most cases a general sense of despondency and despair.[3]

Poverty as a concept is closely related to inequality and may also be identified with unemployment. Given the average income level, higher level of inequality will tend to be associated with a higher level of poverty. Poverty has always had several, not entirely separable meanings and is always defined according to the conventions of the society in which it occurs. In the economic sense it is defined as a state wherein an individual cannot satisfy his minimum needs for healthy living in a given social environment. Many social scientists tend to treat poverty essentially as deprivation, but it has multi-dimensional character. Thus it can be economic, cultural, social or psychological poverty.[4] Martin Rein has defined poverty on the basis of subsistence, inequality and externality concepts. Subsistence is concerned with the minimum provision needed to maintain health and working capacity. Inequality is concerned with relative position of income groups to each other, since the concept of poverty has to be seen in the context of society as a whole. Lastly, externality is concerned with the social consequences of poverty for the rest of the society rather than in terms of the needs of the poor.[5]

There are, however, two major problems involved in defining the concept of poverty. The first relates to the problem of identifying the 'poor' and the second is the problem of measurement. Rowntree was the first in Britain to consider in detail the problems involved in defining poverty, and clearly saw his approach was being based on absolute line. A family was considered to be living in poverty if its total earnings were 'insufficient' to obtain the minimum necessaries for the maintenance of merely physical efficiency.[6] In the United States, Orshansky has given a similar definition of poverty to that of Rowntree's on the basis of the 'estimates' of minimum food expenditure.[7]

TWO CONCEPTS OF POVERTY: RELATIVE AND ABSOLUTE

There are two broad concepts of poverty : relative poverty and absolute poverty, while relative poverty is measured in terms of inequality in the distribution of income, absolute poverty is reckoned in terms of some kind of notion of subsistence considered appropriate to circumstances in the country concerned. The relative poverty prevails even in affluent societies like U.S.A. resultantly the relative differences in income-distribution is an unavoidable circumstance in any society.[8] The concept of absolute poverty attempts to explain the extent of deprivation of resources in a system to one section of the population against the other. This may be explained in terms of disparities in the levels of living prevailing in a society. However, Townsend does not accept the distinction between absolute and relative poverty or between basic and cultural needs, because he argues that the needs which are believed to be basic or absolute can be shown to be relative. He therefore, suggests that poverty must be regarded as general form of relative deprivation, which is the effect of the maldistribution of the resources, and that section of the population whose resources are so depressed from the mean as to be deprived of enjoying the benefits and participating in the activities which are customary in that society can be said to be in poverty.[9]

Bhatty, on the other hand, stated that, both absolute and relative poverty are closely aligned to inequality in income distribution, the relative poverty arises entirely as a consequence of an unequal distribution of income irrespective of what the income level, or the corresponding state of deprivation, of the people at the bottom and of the income scale might be. Absolute poverty on the other hand, expresses a collective view as deprivation in its physical manifestation.[10]

The society may choose any line to separate deprivation from relative comfort, those below the line are defined as poor irrespective of how comfortable or affluent the others may be. Gadgil stated that poverty is nothing but a standard of living below a certain minimum point. After the publication of Rowntree's work the poverty is distinguished as primary and secondary. Primary poverty resulting from inadequate income, and secondary poverty caused by an "ignorant and careless house- keeping and other improvement expenditure" of an adequate income, which leads to degeneration of moral character.[11] According to Marxist, analysis, affluence, and poverty are both the product of capitalist development. Poverty, indeed, is the carcass left from wealth acquisition. [12] In other words, poverty is the product of the capitalist mode of production, the aggrevation of class contradiction in bourgeois society and the rapid growth of the proloteriat.[13]

STUDIES ON POVERTY : AN INDIAN SCENARIO

Studies on poverty in India began with the pioneering work of Dadabai Naoroji in the later part of the 19th century. Naoroji had traced the mass poverty to the British colonial rule which drained out systematically economic amounts of wealth through unequal trade, interest and dividend, salaries and pensions. In the 1930's and 40's Indian scholars, prof. Radha Kamal Mukarji, [14] Gyanchand, [15] and Wadia and Merchant, [16] have drawn attention to the massive and object poverty of the Indian people. However, they did not attempt at any scientific measurement of poverty and its extent in the country. Their studies were not directly related to poverty as such but to problems like food and population or economic and public policies. Perhaps, the first specific and scientific attempt to identify the poor and to measure the extent of poverty was made by an expert committee constituted by the Government of India in July 1962. It has put the nationally desirable minimum level of consumer expenditure at Rs.20 per capita per month according to 1960-61 prices.[17] The figure thus, became and has continued to be the basis of the poverty line. An immediate consequence of this measure was to shift the emphasis from 'poor' country to the 'poor' within the country.

Defining the poverty line has become a controversial issue among the economists and social scientists, not only in India, but in almost all the developing and developed countries also. In developing countries the research on poverty concerned with the incidence of poverty. This provides information on the number of poor at any given time, the extent of their income short fall, and their socio-economic characteristic; but we lack the data of the flow of individuals (or families) into or out of poverty. Such a data will be useful to the planners to have an insight into the poverty and unemployment position and to frame future policies accordingly.[18] As an indicator of poverty, it is desirable to have a data on consumption rather than on income. Firstly, consumption directly measures the flow of utility producing inputs secondly, the use of current consumption as an indicator of poverty is free from the impact of stochastic events (illness, drought etc.,) and of life cycle effects (very young very old age) thirdly, prices may differ substantial across regions, or goods may not the available at the prevailing price, either of which cases would lead to a divergence between distribution of income and distribution of consumption.

We often can't get reliable information on consumption when households are asked how much they consume, a frequent response is, "I spent what I make". Consumption information usually must be obtained from detailed household budget studies, which because of their high administrative costs are not in practice.[19]

The major focus in earlier work on poverty relates to determine the minimum level of living. The study group set up by the Government of India in 1962, deliberated on the question of minimum level of consumer expenditure of Rs. 20 per capita per month at 1960-61 prices. This excludes expenditure on health and education, expected to be provided by the State. Implicit in this expenditure level is a balanced diet recommended by the Nutrition Advisory Committee of the Indian Council of Medical Research (ICMR) in 1958.[20] Further studies are based on the per capita consumption expenditure derived from the intake of per person per day.

The Joint Expert Group [21] of the FAO/WHO (1971) has recommended a minimum of 2223 calories per capita per day for the people in Asia and far East. Minhas (1970) [22] assuming that prices in rural areas are lower than those in the urban areas used a norm of about Rs. 17 per capita per month as the minimum expenditure level for the rural areas. Bardhan (1970) [23] considered Rs. 15 per capita per month as the minimum at 1960-61 prices. In a subsequent study,[24] he uses food basket representing a certain nutritional norms given by Patwardhan with 2100 calories and 55 grams of protein. On this basis he computes the poverty norm at Rs. 11.87 per month for rural poor.

In 1971, Dandekar and Rath introduced the calorie concept explicitly, they considered the energy requirement of 2250 calories as the basic need per day per person. According to them this minimum level of consumption would require an expenditure of Rs. 20 per head per month for rural areas and Rs. 22.50 for urban areas according to 1960-61 prices. Dantwala (1973) stated that there cannot be a single universal norm of poverty. By the official U.S. standards for 1970, a family of 4 members was poor if its income was less than $ 3944 a year. Judged by the same standard probably 99 per cent of India's population could be said to be living in poverty.[25] Hence, one universal norm for measurement of poverty, would be of little help in identifying poverty in each individual country.

According to the Centre for Development Studies (1975),[26] calories norm for Kerala derived from an exercise taking into account the age, sex composition of the states population, turned out to be 2200 calories per day. Sukhatme (1977) [27] would had placed a cut-off point for the Indian population at 2200 calories per person per day. Ahluwalia (1978) [28] used Rs. 180 per annum or Rs. 13 per month per capita to measure the extent of poverty.

In recent years a lively debate on, what should be the cutoff calorie requirement for measuring under-nutrition, for measuring poverty has taken place. The principal participants in the debate are Sukhatme and Dandekar besides many others. The following issues are generally raised in this regard.[29]

1. First, there is a question of defining minimum nutrition requirement in the presence of variability of intakes by the same individual over time. This question raises issues those are essentially biological in nature related to human bodies adjustment to intake and work.

2. Secondly, can one apply a given nutritional norm to judge the extent of under-nourished persons in a highly hetero-geneous population, hetero-geneous by age distribution, activity level, and climatic factors.

P.V. Sukhatme [30] challenges the theory that nutritional requirement for an individual are fixed. He argues that the requirements lie within a range. He derives his argument from the experimental data on energy in-take of the army recruits. The data shows that, there is considerable variation in energy in-take. While analysing the variations in intakes he finds that intra-personal variation is the major and most fundamental source of variation. He also asserts that the daily energy intake may not equal expenditures. The body regulates its energy balance either by varying the intake or expenditure or both. He further argues that individuals can sustain themselves at energy intakes much below the average without effecting their body weight.

Krishnaji [31] reacts to the calorie norm for estimating poverty from the NSS data. How do we apply this cut-off point to a given distribution of intakes in a hetero-geneous population. The hetero-genity in NSS data could be removed through an appropriate conversion of persons or house holds into standard consumer units. This requires knowledge about age, sex, and the level of activity.

Dandekar compares Sukhatme's contention to Say's law of markets. Say's law, according to Dandekar, can be said to be true, due to a self-regulatory mechanism of adjustment between saving and investment, if the process of adjustment and the cost of adjustment in the form of varying levels of economic activity and employment are ignored. In the case of nutrition level also, the body may self-regulate and achieve a balance but it does so at a very low level of out-put and productivity.[32] Paranjape supports Dandekar's argument and cites evidence from the nutrition literature in support of the point that adoption to nutritional inadequacy, if achieved, is at the cost of functional competence and efficiency. [33] Gopalan, in a similar veiw, writes .... "adoption of this kind ...... can only perpetuate the status quo of poor communities. It can't lead to their development and progress, and therefore, is undesirable".[34]

Mitra suggests, "it is quite possible that if calorieprotein intake were increased among the L.D.C.s, the people would become as restless, innovative migratory and colonists as any Northern European Nations. Wouldn't the Government be quite happy to forget about such potentialities and accept Sukhatme's approach to re-define poverty"[35]?

This discussion clearly shows that measuring the poverty on the basis of calorie intake has its advantages and disadvantages. Though Dandekar, Paranjape and others have tried to enhance the importance of calorie intake norm but the whole range of other components of poverty cannot be ignored. It must consider access to clothing, housing, health, education and atleast some leisure and leisure time activities. It is essential to include other nutrients, such as Protein, Calcium, Iron and Vitamin 'A'. Keeping this in view, it is necessary to develop a scale which express the people's condition in terms of physical quality of life. Alpin has developed a scale called PQLI (physical quality of life index) to measure the poor condition of people of a particular country or place.

The minimum calorie intake of 2400 calories per person per day for rural areas and 2100 calories for the urban areas was adopted by the Planning Commission. (1978-83). By including expenditure on non-food items, the cut-off points in the consumer expenditure data turn out to be Rs. 61-8 and Rs. 71.3 per capita per month for rural and urban areas respectively at 1976-77 prices. On the basis of the same requirements the revised Sixth Plan (1980-85) defined poverty line in terms of 1979-80 prices as per capita monthly expenditure of Rs. 76 for rural areas and Rs. 88 for urban.

II

'Development' has traditionally been associated with high rates of growth in aggregate and per capita incomes. In the earlier approaches to development problems, emphasis was laid on aggregate rates of growth of domestic product. "We were confidently told to take care of G.N.P. and poverty will take care of itself, that a high G.N.P. growth target is the best guarantee for eliminating unemployment and redistributing incomes later through physical means".[36] But the gradual realisation that economic growth has bypassed the large percentage of population in the developing countries led to the awareness that growth in average G.N.P. is not a reliable indicator of improvements in economic well-being. [37] Further massive increase in unemployment observed in the developing countries in the face of rapid population growth and the resulting erosion in the levels of living led development analysts to question the erstwhile strategies of growth.[38] It has become evident that economic growth, to be meaningful should reach the masses as it is the only meaningful way of transferring purchasing power and raising the general level of well-being.[39] In this connection Mahabub-Ul-Haq observes, "the basic problem of development should be redefined as a selective attack on the worst forms of poverty, hence take care of poverty as this will take care of G.N.P."[40]

Dandekar and Rath [41] stated that the problem of poverty in India is a problem of low national-income and its unequal distribution, of slow pace of development and inequitable distribution of small gains of development. Madalgi [42] opined that the poverty of the masses in India is reflected in the extent of their under nourishment. Much of this poverty is concentrated in rural India, particularly in areas where there is high concentration of landless labourers.

After the advent of independence, sustained attempts have been made at planned development and the elimination of structural constraints in improving the living levels of the masses.[43] Conscious efforts were made from time to time to estimate the extent of poverty, primarily taking the per capita consumption expenditure as the base. B.S.Minhas, on the basis of the figures recommended by the study group estimated that 65 percent of population was below the minimum levels of living in the year 1956-57 and 50.6 in 1967-68. [44].

P.D.Ojha [45] has estimated the number of persons below the poverty line on the basis of an average caloric in take of 2250 per capita per day. This entailed monthly per capita consumption expenditure of Rs.15 to 18 (1960-61 price) in urban areas and of Rs.8 to 11 in rural areas. On this basis, Ojha estimated 51.8 percent of the rural population and 7.6 percent of urban population below the poverty line in 1960-61. For 1967-68 he estimated that 289 million persons (70 percent of the rural population) lived below the poverty line.

Using N.S.S. data based on the monthly per capita expenditure for the year 1963-64, Da costa [46] of the Indian Institute of Public Opinion classified the rural poor into three categories viz; the severe destitute, the destitute and the poor. As per his estimates 62 million persons live a life of severe destitution and 104 million of destitution and 162 million of poverty.

Bardhan's [47] results are in direct contrast to those of Minhas using a different minimum level of income of Rs.15 per capita per month for rural area and Rs.21 for urban areas at 1960-61 prices. He estimated that 38 percent (135 million persons) in rural areas, 44 percent (34 million people) in urban areas fall below the poverty line in 1960-61. Bardhan further stated that in 1968- 69 (at 1960-61 prices) as many as 54 percent of rural population and 41 percent of urban population fall below the poverty line. Thus, Bardhan's time series study showed a sharp rise in the incidence of poverty overtime in both the rural and urban areas.

Dandekar and Rath [48] used the N.S.S. estimates of consumption of food-grains without any correction, and assumed a yield of 2250 calories per capita per day from other items of food. By working out annual per capita consumer expenditure of Rs.170.8 for rural areas and Rs.271.7 for urban areas in 1960-61 prices, estimated 33.12 percent of the rural population and 48.64 percent of the urban population would have been living below the level of poverty in the year 1960-61. Considering a per capita annual expenditure of Rs.324 in rural areas and Rs.486 in urban areas, (at 1968-69 prices) as necessary for a minimum level of living, Dandekar and Rath estimated 40 percent of the rural population and 50 percent of the urban population are found to be living below the desirable minimum level.

Vaidyanathan [49] by using Rs.21.44 as average per capita consumption per month at 1960-61 prices finds that about 67.9 percent of the rural population was living in poverty in 1967-68.

Bhatty [50] adopted both Sen's poverty index and traditional head count in quantifying the incidence of poverty among the various rural occupational groups and found the incidence to be maximum among the agricultural labourers (89.56%) followed by non-agricultural worker (78.77%) and cultivators (70.28%) for the year 1968-69.

Mukerji [51] prepared a map of India, delineating clusters of regions relatively homogeneous in respect of level of living and incidence of poverty. According to the per capita expenditure he formed a group comprising the poorest 10 percent of India's rural population and then examined how many of these poor fell in different regions. Judging both the rural and urban segments of the States as a whole on the criteria of density of the poor and per capita expenditure, he found Orissa, Kerala, Bihar, Mysore and Andhra Pradesh among the poorer states in 1963-64.

Serious attempts have been made by the planners to eradicate the extent of poverty. In the Fifth Five Year Plan it was stated that "the existence of poverty is incompatible with the vision of an advanced, prosperous, democratic and just society implied in the concept of a socialist pattern of development. In fact, it holds a potential threat to the unity, integrity and independence of the country. Elimination of poverty must, therefore, have the highest priority".[52] The Fifth Plan stated "at present over 220 millions are estimated to be living below the poverty line.[53] The revised Sixth Five Year Plan (1980-85) defined poverty line in terms of 1979-80 prices as per capita monthly expenditure of Rs. 76 for rural areas and Rs.88 for urban areas. On this basis the Sixth Five Year Plan (1980-85) estimated as 370 million persons are living below the poverty line. Out of them 260 million are from rural areas and 57 million from urban areas in relative terms 50.7 percent of rural population and 40 percent of the urban population is classed as "the poor". Taking the country as a whole, 48.4 percent of the people live below the poverty line.[54]

After reviewing all the earlier studies on poverty, the Seventh Plan tried to have a fresh look at the problem by using 32 round (N.S.S. data)on consumer expenditure (1977-78) and also consumer expenditure distribution of 38th round (N.S.S. Provisional) 1983-84, which estimated the population below the poverty line in 1984-85 at 33.9 (222.2 million persons) percent in rural area and 27.3 (50.5 million persons) percent in urban. [55] Taking India as a whole 36.9 percent (272.7 million) of the total population was living below the poverty line. The Seventh Plan document projected to bring down the population below the poverty line from 272.7 million in 1984-85 to 211 million in 1989-90. It further stated to bring down the rural poverty in particular from 40 percent in 1984-85 to around 28 percent by 1990 and to reduce this percentage further to 10 by 1995. [56]

In the Table-2.1 the Planning Commission estimates are derived by using the poverty line of Rs. 49.00 per capita per month at 1973- 74 prices corresponding to daily calorie requirement of 2400 per person in rural areas and the poverty line of Rs. 56.64 per capita per month corresponding to calories requirement of 2100 in urban areas. C.S.O. poverty consumption data has been used for updating the poverty line for 1983-84 and the results are based on the provisional and quick tabulation of the N.S.S. on household consumer expenditure of 38th Round (January 1983 to December 1983). The difference between the aggregate all India private consumption expenditure estimated by Central Statistical Organisation in their National Accounts Statistics and that derived from the N.S.S.O. data has been adjusted among different States and Union Territories in the absence of any information to allocate the difference among the States and

Union Territories. The N.S.S. estimates of percentage people below
the poverty line is worked out from the N.S.S. reports on consumer
expenditure for 1977- 78 and 1983.

Table - 2.1

PERCENTAGE OF PEOPLE BELOW THE POVERTY LINE,
1977-78 AND 1983-84

| STATES | 1977 - 78 | | | | 1983 - 84 | | | |
| | Rural | | Urban | | Rural | | Urban | |
	N.S.S.	Planning Commission	N.S.S.	Planning Commission	NSS	Planning Commission	N.S.S.	Planning Commission
A.P.	54	45	46	37	48	39	38	21
Assam	N.A	49	N.A	N.A	46	24	35	22
Bihar	49	58	37	45	58	51	43	37
Gujarat	47	43	33	30	42	28	31	17
J & K	49	32	56	41	45	16	43	16
Haryana	N.A	23	N.A	N.A	22	15	123	17
Karnataka	55	53	44	45	52	38	42	29
Kerala	49	47	55	53	51	26	53	30
M.P	62	62	47	47	60	50	42	31
Maharastra	64	60	34	31	56	42	34	23
Orissa	76	68	49	42	74	45	56	29
Punjab	N.A	13	N.A	N.A	16	11	26	22
Rajasthan	35	34	36	34	48	37	29	26
Tami Nadu	66	56	54	45	69	44	56	31
U.P	49	50	49	49	55	47	48	40
W.Bengal	62	58	38	34	61	45	40	27
All-India	53	51	40	38	55	40	40	28

Source : National Accounts Statistice Revised Series
(February, 1988)

REVIEW OF POVERTY LEVELS IN ANDHRA PRADESH

Micro-level studies on poverty on the basis of consumption expenditure are available from pioneering works done by Ravi Verma,[57] Sinha,[58] Kumar,[59] Gupta,[60] Maitra,[61] Radhakrishna,[62] and Mishra and Mahajan.[63] All these studies focussed their attention on regional variation in poverty levels. These studies are immensely valuable in working out micro-level planning for various regions which in turn strengthen the machinery involved in poverty eradication and for overall economic growth. As the incidence of poverty has its roots in the endowment of resources and their proper utilisation, agro-climatic conditions and unemployment which vary from region to region, there is every necessity to study regional pattern of poverty levels.

Dr. B.Someshwar Rao [64] (1973), attributes three major reasons for the low level of living in rural areas: (i) the highly unequal distribution of land and high incidence of tenancy and high rents (ii) the low rate of real wages and the negligible trend of rise in it and (iii) the inadequate reinvestment of the economic surplus within the area, which itself arises from the unequal distribution of land and the income from land.

G.Parthasarathi [65] and others (1973) conducted a sample study of "Employment and Unemployment of rural labour in West Godavari District, revealed that 62 percent of the households are found to be poor and unemployed. Further, 86 percent of landless labourers and 68 percent among landed laboureres are found to be below the poverty line on the basis of Rs. 450 per capita annual income in 1971-72 prices.

Perraju Sharma's study on "Dimensions of Rural Poverty" in an agriculturally developed district viz., Krishan district in A.P. reveals that the incidence of poverty is 41 percent for all households, 47 percent for landless labour households and 26 percent for landed labour households among the sample households.[66]

K. Hanumantha Rao and K.V.S. Sastri,[67] worked out the incidence of poverty in rural Andhra Pradesh on the basis of head-count ratio and calculated the poverty index adopting Chakravarthy's method (1983). The average per capita monthly expenditure of Rs. 81.00 for rural Andhra Pradesh has been adopted as an indicator of level of living. The inter-regional difference indicate that, in general, the standard of living is low in Rayalaseema and high in Coastal Andhra and Telengana occupying the middle position. This study, concentrated on social-group-wise comparisons, reveals that the standard of living is consistently higher in respect of O.C. followed by B.C. Barring a few cases, the S.Ts are placed on the lower rung of the ladder of the living standards.[68]

A comprehensive study was made by Prof. R.Radhakrishna [69] (1988) on the basis of 32nd round N.S.S. data on the levels of living in the different districts of Andhra Pradesh. The total consumer expenditure of Andhra Pradesh in 1977-78 was worked out to Rs. 35,570 millions of which rural areas account for 71 percent and urban areas 29 percent. Per-capita monthly expenditure was estimated as Rs. 58.18 for Andhra Pradesh, Rs. 53.25 was worked out to rural areas and Rs. 75.49 for urban. "The districtwise per capita monthly expenditure estimates, reveals that, in the case of rural areas, Krishna, Guntur and East- Godavari in Coastal Andhra, Nalgonda and Khammam in Telengana are at the top in per capita expenditure, while Srikakulam (Coastal Andhra) Ananthapur (Rayalaseema) and Karimnagar, Warangal, Adilabad and Medak (Telanagana) are at the bottom".[70] It is significant to observe that the average per capita expenditure of the bottom districts is less than Rs. 50 per month; i.e. poverty line adopted in this study for rural areas. In the case of urban areas, Vishakhapatnam of Coastal Andhra, Nalgonda and Hyderabad of Telangana are at the top; while Cuddapah of Rayalaseema; and Karimnagar, Warangal and Adilabad of Telangana are at the bottom. Considering rural and urban areas together Krishna, East- Godavari, West-Godavari and Vishakhapatnam of Coastal Andhra, Nalgonda and Hyderabad of Telangana occupy top positions. While Srikakulam of Coastal Andhra, Ananthapur of Rayalaseema and Karimnagar, Medak, Mahabubnagar, Warangal and Adilabad of Telangana gravitate towards the bottom.

Districtwise poverty magnitudes in the rural areas is shown in the Table-2.2. The Table-2.3 contains data relating to the poverty levels of rural population of districts based on class structure.

The evidence supports the earlier assertion that the poverty levels are comparatively low in 'employed' non-agricultural class. Rayalaseema provides the most striking examples for class difference in poverty. In general, poverty magnitudes are higher for agricultural labourers both in developed and less developed districts. On the other hand, in rural areas development appears to have made a dent on the poverty levels among cultivators and self employed non-agricultural class.

Table -2.2
POVERTY LEVELS IN RURAL ANDHRA PRADESH IN 1977-78

DISTRICTS	Percentage of persons below poverty line	Percentage of house-holds below poverty line	Estimated number of persons below poverty line (in lakhs)	Estimated number of households below poverty line (in lakhs)
Srikakulam	71.93	68.74	17.49	3.51
Visakapatnam	59.02	53.36	14.07	2.95
East Godavari	50.19	44.56	13.93	2.93
West Godavari	42.09	35.08	9.18	1.85
Krishna	37.11	32.93	7.37	1.59
Guntur	35.99	31.43	8.60	1.79
Prakasam	47.96	44.90	8.59	2.06
Nellore	47.84	39.91	7.33	11.27
Chittor	52.04	49.36	11.44	2.15
Cuddapah	51.30	43.98	7.70	1.32
Ananthapur	69.57	67.64	13.87	2.83
Kurnool	66.04	61.89	11.58	0.94
Mahabubnagar	64.00	60.21	13.22	2.28
Hyderabad	61.93	57.29	7.02	1.51
Medak	71.22	67.54	10.96	2.32
Nizamabad	41.70	41.62	5.37	1.04
Adilabad	74.60	65.80	9.51	1.92
Karimnagar	78.61	76.98	15.92	3.16
Warangal	72.80	69.79	13.32	3.89
Khammam	37.80	36.96	5.22	0.90
Nalgonda	29.93	27.38	5.78	1.03

Note : Poverty line Rs. 50.00 per month

Source : Levels of living in a State setting CESS, Hyderabad.

Table - 2.3
POVERTY LEVELS OF RURAL SUB-POPULATION AND HOUSE-HOLDS IN 1977-78

DISTRICTS	Cultivators		Agricultural Labourers		Self Employed non-agricultural Population		Employed non-agricultural population	
	Percentage of persons below poverty line	Percentage of Households below poverty line	Percentage of persons below poverty line	Percentage of Households below povety line	Percentage of persons below poverty line	Percentage of Households below poverty line	Percentage of persons below poverty line	Percentage of Households below poverty line
Srikakulam	58.45	55.32	90.63	84.57	65.94	62.92	73.02	60.00
Visakapatnam	51.04	46.49	73.89	65.73	52.39	46.51	45.00	25.00
East Godavari	25.92	21.15	62.97	54.60	48.81	41.30	21.43	21.43
West Godavari	21.00	18.52	57.97	45.41	38.34	31.11	23.08	16.67
Krishna	23.00	20.60	47.52	40.19	61.60	28.26	30.38	32.00
Guntur	6.44	5.34	55.38	45.25	42.42	36.79	25.40	18.75
Prakasam	29.63	26.17	73.31	68.28	45.51	35.90	28.57	20.00
Nellore	35.29	31.34	61.70	50.00	32.26	22.72	27.54	22.22
Chittor	34.80	32.65	72.34	65.14	52.72	47.45	27.02	25.00
Cuddapah	48.08	40.78	63.28	53.00	40.72	40.90	30.00	21.05
Ananthapur	58.73	56.49	91.64	85.61	71.65	68.29	19.70	25.00
Kurnool	53.29	51.16	85.95	78.98	54.64	49.32	52.94	27.27
Mahabubnagar	57.85	55.10	71.30	66.67	67.32	60.76	41.46	40.00
Hyderabad	47.65	41.77	86.38	80.56	60.84	51.51	34.29	25.30
Medak	62.83	59.65	88.34	80.77	74.14	69.49	60.87	52.94
Nizamabad	38.54	38.14	64.12	62.07	22.42	25.00	-	-
Adilabad	69.93	63.64	91.99	83.16	61.11	44.90	37.50	14.29
Karimnagar	68.52	63.83	90.70	87.25	77.28	79.49	75.51	80.00
Warangal	58.93	55.06	95.83	90.43	74.85	69.66	60.87	66.67
Khammam	30.46	27.91	55.85	56.67	28.35	26.87	14.03	14.29
Nalgonda	16.34	15.53	48.90	44.78	29.29	24.04	33.77	23.81

Note : Poverty line Rs. 50.00 per month

In the Table 2.3 the districts with high poverty level in various occupational classes are identified by taking the 55 percent as the cut off point. The table shows that while the poor of agricultural labour population are spatially spread over the entire Andhra Pradesh, the poor among the other classes are concentrated in less developed districts.

The above study concludes that agricultural development does not make much dent on the poverty of agricultural labour class which constitutes the hard core of the poor. There appears to be a systematic relationship between agricultural development and occupational composition of rural households. The size of agricultural labour class increases with advent of development, while that of the cultivator class declines. For instance, agricultural labour households account for as high as 60 percent of the rural households in the agriculturally developed district viz; East-Godavari while it accounts for only 29 percent of the rural households in agriculturally backward district i.e. Medak. On the other hand, cultivator households constitute only 19 percent in East-Godavari, while the proportion is as high as 43 percent in Medak. The same tendency is reflected in the occupational composition of other districts also.

On the basis of study made by Radhakrishna and associates, we can draw up the position of Warangal District in A.P. regarding per capita monthly expenditure, Gross National Product and Poverty levels.

The above table clearly reveals that Warangal District is in the lower position both in per capita expenditure and per capita Gross Domestic Product. It has been ranked with 20th position in per capita expenditure as well as in per capita G.D.P. Regarding poverty levels also the Warangal District position among other districts is so pathetic that 72.80 per cent of rural population is below the poverty line. Warangal District has been ranked number 3 in descending order, 58.93 percentage of cultivators, 95.83 percentage of agricultural laboureres, 74.87 percent of self-employed non-agricultural population and 60.87 percent of employed non-agricultural population are living below the poverty line.

Table - 2.4
GROUPING OF DISTRICTS BY LEVELS OF DEVELOPMENT AND PER CAPITA EXPENDITURE

Per capita GDP	Per capita Exp. Top	Middle	Bottom
Top	KSN,HYD	WGL,NZB NLR,KNL. PKM	
Middle	NLG,EG GNT,VSP	CTR	ATP,ADB
Bottom	KHM	CDP	SKL,MDK, MBR,KRM, WGL

Source: Levels of living in a state setting p.23

REFERENCE

1. Hanumappa H.G   :   Dimensions of Rural Poverty in India,
                             New-Delhi 1979, p. 140

2. Kurian C.T   :   Poverty, Planning and Social
                             Transformation, Bombay 1978, p.8
                             Allied Publishers

3. Josheph S.E   :   A strategy to eradicate rural poverty,
                             Yojana Oct., 16, 1978, p. 20

4. Town Send Peter   :   Measures and explorations of poverty
                             in high income and low income
                             countries, is the concept of poverty,
                             Heinemann, London, 1970

5. Rein Martin   :   Problems is the definition and
                             measurement of poverty: In Town Send,
                             Heinem, London 1970, p. 46

6. Rowntree B.S   :   Poverty-A study of life, Ma Millan,
                             1928, quoted in A.B. Atkinson, the
                             economics of inequality p.126

7. Orshnasky M   :   Counting the poor: Antother look at the
                             poverty profile, Social Security Bulletin,
                             28, quoted in A.B. Atkinson, the
                             economics of inequality, Oxford
                             University Press, 1975

8. Amatyasen   :   op-cit p-69

9. Townsend Peter   :   op-cit p.p.-2, 19,42

10. Bhatta I.J : "Inequality and poverty in rural India." In T.N. Srinivasan and P.K. Bardhan (ed) op-cit p.292

11. Gadgil D.R : Sholapur City: Socio-economic Studies, Asia Publishing House, 1965 P.p-233-234

12. Kurian C.T : op-cit p-8

13. Sdobniova, Galina : Scientific Communism, Progress Publisher, 1982 p-22

14. : Food Planning for 400 millions, Bombay 1938

15. : India's teming millions, Delhi 1939

16. : Our Economic Problem, Bombay 1943

17. Kurian C.T : op-cit p-11

18. Gary S.Fields : Poverty, inequality and development, Cambridge University Press, Cambridge 1980 p-141

19. Gary S.Fields : op-cit p-142

20. Sengupta S and Joshi P.D : On the concept of poverty line and the estimate of poverty at the regional level in India (mimeo) 1981

21. F.A.O. : Agricultural Commodity Projections, 1970-80 Rome 1971, p-31

22. Minhas B.S   :   Rural Poverty, Land Redistribution
                            and Development strategy: Facts and
                            Policy, Indian Economic Review, Vol. 5
                            1970 p-p 97-128

23. Bardhan P.K   :   "Green revolution and agricultural
                            labourers", EPW Vol. 5 1970, reprinted
                            in Srikanth Sambrani, Ed: Rural
                            Development for Weaker Section,
                            Bombay 1974, p.p-23-39

24. Bardhan P.K   :   'On the incidence of poverty in Rural
                            India in the 60's', EPW Vol.8 VIII
                            Annual No. February 1973

25. Dantwala M.L   :   Poverty in India: Then and now,
                            1870-1970, the Mac Millan Company of
                            India Ltd., New-Delhi 1973 p-16

26. Centre for
    Development Studies :   Poverty, Unemployment and
                            Development Policy: A case study of
                            selected issues with refcrecne to
                            Kerala, United Nations, Newyork,
                            1975, p-32

27. Sukhatme P.V   :   "Incidence of Under-Nutrition", Indian
                            Journal of Agricultural Economics,
                            July-Sept. 1977. p-7

28. Montech.S.
    Ahluwalia   :   "Rural Poverty and Agricultural
                            Performance in India". The Journal of
                            Development Studies, April. 1978
                            p-89-92.

29. Sukhatme P.V : 'Relationship between malnutrition and poverty', First Natinal Conference on 'Social Science and the Problem of Poverty', Indian Association of Social Science Institutions, New-Delhi, January 12-15, 1981

30. Sukhatme P.V : op-cit.

31. Krishnaji.N : On measuring incidence of undernutrition what is a consumer unit? EPW Vol. XXVI No. 37, 1981 1942.

32. Dandekar V.M : 'On measurement of poverty, EPW Vol. XXVI No. 30, 1981 1325.

33. Paramjepe M.K : How poor are we? EPW Vol. XXVI, No. 36 Sept., 5 1981 p.1471

34. Gopalan C : 'Adoption to Low Calories and Low Protiens Intake Does it Exit? In Margan. S. and Ogar, R.A. Programmes in Human Nutrition, Vol. II 1978.

35. Mitra Ashok : "Revolution by re-definition of parameters": In progress in Human Nutrition, Vol, II 1978, pp 297-305; Quoted by Parmajape op-cit.

36. Mahabub-UI-Haq : "Employment and income distribution in the 70s -new perspective", Development Digest October 1971.

37. Siman Kuznets : Population, capital and growth, W.W. Nortan Co. New-York 1973.

38. Baer W and
    Harwell,H   :   "Employment and Industrialisation in
                                Developing Countries". Quarterly
                                Journal of Economics, 1966. P.P. 88-89.

39. Nirmal Kumar Bose   :   Selections from Gandhi, Navajeevan
                                Publication House, Ahmedabad, 1957
                                P.P. 46-48.

40. Mahabub-Ul-Haq   :   op-cit

41. Dandekar V.M
    and Rath   :   Poverty in India, Indian School of
                                Political Economy, 1971, Bombay p. 1

42. Madalgi S.S   :   "Hunger in rural India: 1960-61 to 64-65
                                EPW Annual No. January 1968. p.63.

43. Dalip S. Thakur   :   op. cit p.70.

44. Minhas B.S   :   Rural poverty, Land Pre-Distributions
                                and Development",Indian Economic
                                Review, Vol V No. 1 April 1970:
                                reprinted. in Sankya, series C, Vol 36
                                1974 p.p.252-263.

45. Ojha P.D   ·   "A configaration of Indian poverty,
                                inequality and levels of living", RBI
                                Bulletin January 1970.

46. Ruddar Dutt &
    Sundaram K.P.M   :   Indian economy, S.Chand & Co Ltd.
                                New-Delhi 1985 p. 287.

47. Bardhan P.K   :   "On the Minimum Level of Living and
                               the Rural Poor", Indian Economic
                               Review 1970.

48. Dandekar & Rath   :   op cit p.150

49. Vaidyanathan.A   :   Some Aspects of Inequalitities in Living
                               Standards in Rural India, in Poverty
                               and Income Distribution in India(ed)
                               T.N.Srinivasan and P.K. Bardhan
                               Statistical Publishing Society, Calcutta
                               1974 p.p. 215-241.

50. Bhatt.I.J   :   Inequality and Poverty in Rural India
                               and Income Distribution in India,
                               edited by T.N.Srinivasan, P.K.Bardhan,
                               Statistical Publishing Society, Calcutta,
                               1974, p.p. 291-336.

51. Mukerji   :   "Size and area distribution of the level
                               of living in India", Sankya series B 31,
                               Parts 3,4 1964 p.p. 459-478.

52. Planning Commission: Draft Fifth Five Year Plan Vol.1 p.6.

53. Ibid   :   p.9

54. Planning Commission: Sixth Five Year Plan(1980-85) Chapter
                               15

55. Planning Commission: Seventh Five Year Plan 1985-90 Vol. 1
                               perspective, objectives, strategy,
                               macro-dimensions and resources 1985.

56. Kurian N.J   :   Anti-poverty programme: A
                            reappraisal. EPW March 25, 1989
                            p.A.15.

57. Ravi Verma   :   "Income Elasticity of Foodgrains",
                            Artha Vijnana Vol. 1. 1959. p.p.271-280.

58. Sinha R.P   :   "Analysis of Food Expenditure in
                            India", Journal of Farm Economics
                            Vol.48, 1966 p.113 to 123.

59. Kumar   :   "Income Elasticity of Demand". A
                            regional analysis, Artha Vijnana Vol.9
                            1967. p.p. 184-195.

60. Gupta D.V   :   "A comparison of consumption
                            patterns in U.P. and Madras-A study of
                            inter-regional variation with references
                            to India", Indian Economic Review,
                            (New series),Vol 3,1968. p.p.129-144.

61. Mitra,T   :   "On Regional and Temporal Engel
                            Curves in Rural India," Technical
                            Report, Eco. No. 2,1969, p.69

62. Radha Krishna.R
    and Mishra G.K   :   "A Regional Approach to the
                            Consumption Patterns of India", Artha
                            Vijnana, Vol.12.p.p.532-62, 1970.

63. Mahajan.B.M   :   "Inter-regional homoegenity of
                            consumer behaviour in India", Artha
                            Vijnana, 1971 pp.1-37.

64. Sarveshwar Rao.B : "Productivity, Employment and Poverty in Rural area", a study of agriculturally advanced area in A.P., Madras Institute of Development Studies, Somaiya Publications Pvt. Ltd. Bombay, 1982. pp.52-75.

65. Parthasarathi.G.
    Venkateshwar Rao,S
    & Dashartha
    Rama Rao.G   : "Character of Poverty and Rural Poor", Madras Institute of Development Studies, Somaiya Publications Pvt. Ltd. Bombay 1982 PP.33-39.

66. Perraju Sharma   : Dimensions

67. Hanumanth Rao.K
    & Shastri.K.V.S   : "Levels of living and poverty among social-groups in Andhra Pradesh": A cross section analysis, Journal of Rural Development Vol.9(1) NIRD Hyderabad.1990.pp.91 to 105.

68. Ibid   : P.20-21

69. Radha Krishna.R.
    Shastry,S.A.R   : "Levels of Living in a State Setting", Centre for Economic and Social Studies, Sudhakar Reddy.S. Hyderabad and Concept Publishing & Mitra.G.K. Company New-Delhi,1988 p.10.

70. Ibid   : P.39.

3

POVERTY ERADICATION PROGRAMMES : A REVIEW

Though in India experimentation for intervention in the rural sector for increasing agricultural productivity and generally raising the standard of living of the rural masses has been on since the days of Community Development in the 1950's, distinct focus was given to these programmes at the end of the sixties and in the beginning of seventies.[1] A number of policy measures were initiated in the interest of the small and marginal farmers, agricultural labourers, artisans, scheduled castes and tribes and for the development of neglected areas. As the growth in agricultural production has not been associated with an improvement in the levels of living of the rural poor, it has become imperative to the Government(s) to evolve multi-pronged programmes to benefit the neglected masses.

There are two basic pre-requisites of a poverty eradication programme. Firstly, reorientation of the agrarian relations, so that the ownership of land is shared by a larger section of population. Besides this, the tenancy rights provide security to the cultivating classes. Various studies and experience of many countries proved that small holdings are achieving high productivity per unit of land. Hence, the distribution of surplus land to large number of small cultivators [2] may not pose any technological problem.

Secondly, no programme of poverty eradication can succeed in an economy plagued by inflation and spiralling rise of prices. Inflation by it's very nature accentuates inequalities, erodes the income of the poor classes and thus, leads to a deterioration in their economic condition.

Production oriented approach of planning should alter the mode of production to solve the problem of poverty and inequality. In this connection the draft of the Fifth Plan status that "in elaborating our strategy of development in earlier plan documents, we seem to have assumed that a fast rate of growth of national income will by itself create more and fuller employment and provide high living standards for poor".[3] The philosophy of automatic transmission (trickle down strategy), of the benefits arising from an increase in production to huge needy masses has been a failure. It is now a well accepted proposition that growth by itself may not contribute to the reduction of poverty, unless the existing structural deficiencies are removed and productive assets are made more equitable, by reducing sharp inequalities in the ownership of assets and access to resources and technology.[4]

Two conferences of chief ministers took place in 1971 and 1972 which deliberated on the agrarian unrest prevailing at that time and formulated National Policy of Land Reforms. Simultaneously, SFDA, Command Area Development Programme (CADP), Drought Prone Area Programmes were started in Fourth-Five-Year Plan. Food for Work Programme and Desert Development Programme were introduced in the Fifth Plan, but by and large, these Programmes were ad-hoc in nature with its own line of administration without much of coordination and any conceptual frame of complementarity in which they were to operate.[5] The Sixth Five Year Plan in a way, by passed earlier ad-hocism in its candid appreciation of the poverty issue. By recognising that the earlier sporadic and often transient measures left untouched the lower strata of the rural poor, i.e. the landless and rural artisans, the Sixth Five Year Plan prescribed that households below the poverty line, have to be assisted with an appropriate package of skill development technologies, services and productive asset transfer programme and wage employment. It has envisaged a direct attack on poverty and unemployment with target group oriented programmes of income generation through productive asset and skill endowment and direct supplemental wage employment through public works. Programmes for special areas to counter endemic poverty caused by hostile agro-climatic conditions and degeneration of eco-systems, were proposed. As back-up support to the poverty groups, Minimum Needs Programme was also initiated to improve the quality of life of the poorest and to give infrastructural support to other programmes of poverty alleviation. Integrated Rural Development Programme (IRDP), Training for Rural Youth for Self Employment (TRYSEM), Development of Women and Children in Rural Areas (DWCRA), National Rural Employment Programme (NREP) and Rural Landless Employment Guarantee Programme (RLEGP) were started in this plan.

In the above package, the most important productive asset that ought to be given to the rural poor as a support to any activity, the land, was missing. In the Seventh Five Year Plan, there has been a positive conceptual change. The approach to the Seventh Five Year Plan (1985-90) states, "the core of the anti-poverty programmes lies in the endowment of income generating assets on those who have little or none of this. Hence, redistributive land reform and security of tenure have to be directly integrated with the anti-poverty package of programme".[6] It also observes "Land Reforms have been recognised to constitute a vital element both in terms of anti-poverty strategy and for modernisation and increased productivity in agriculture. Redistribution of land could provide a permanent asset base for large number of rural landless poor for taking up land based and other allied activities".[7] Though, the Seventh Plan, has brought land reforms into the mainstream of rural development activity, it is still a long way to integrate it operationally with the other programmes, and no specific programme has been initiated in this direction. As a "new wine in old bottle", the Jawahar Rojgar Yojana by merging NREP and RLEGP programmes was introduced in 1989.

A concerted attempt has been made in the following pages to review some of the anti-poverty programmes initiated by the Government from time to time in the Five Year Plans.

1. SMALL FARMERS DEVELOPMENT AGENCY (SFDA)

The Utter failure of the "trickle down agency" (CDP,IADP,IAAP and HYVP)to produce any visible impact on the economic condition of the weaker sections led to the adoption of a target group approach from the Fourth Five Year Plan. The objective was to create a direct impact on the economic status of the rural poor. It started with Small Farmers Development Agency and has multiplied since then. The much publicised Integrated Rural Development Programme of these days is a direct off-shoot of the SFDA.

The Small Farmers Development Agency was established on the basis of the recommendation made by All India Rural Credit Review Committee in 1969, to assist the small farmers who were not benefited from the then existing programmes. The Committee recommended to set up special institutions of SFDA in selected districts for giving support to small farmers in terms of credit, technical guidance etc. Initially , 46 SFDA pilot projects were started during the Fourth Plan. On the recommendation of National Commission on Agriculture, MFAL agencies were merged with SFDA. Later, in 1979 SFDA was extended to 198 districts, before it was merged with the IRDP. The main objectives of the SFDA were: (i) to identify the members of the target groups and their problems, (ii) to draw up and execute plans for investment and production in respect of activities which might be taken up by them for their own benefit (iii) apart from providing subsidies and arranging loans, the SFDA was required to organise and arrange for supplies of inputs; such as fertilisers, seeds and pesticides, agricultural implements, marketing services and other facilities to small and marginal farmers, and (iv) to review the progress and effectiveness there of.[9] Upto September 1977, the SFDA received a budgetary support to the tune of Rs. 134.31 crores, of which Rs. 123.59 crores was given out as credit to over 6 million households.[10]

2. INTEGRATED RURAL DEVELOPMENT PROGRAMME (IRDP)

To integrate various programmes that were initiated earlier for rural development into a compact programme to deliver desirable results more effectively and to strengthen various agencies involved in rural upliftment, the IRD programme was introduced in 1978-79, initially, in 2300 blocks and in October 1980 it was extended to all the blocks in the country to provide self- employment opportunities to the rural poor to uplift them above the poverty line. The main objective of IRDP is to enable the subsistance families to cross the poverty line. The Sixth Plan states, " it is important that the identification of an economic activity for a house-hold is done in full consultation with beneficiary house-hold concerned so that the project is appropriate to its inclination and management capability. The project must also be able to give net income to take it across the poverty line". IRD programme is a family based, beneficiary oriented programme. Asserting the importance of IRD programme the draft of the Sixth Five Year Plan (1978-83) stated, "the imperative laid down for the plan for rural areas of the country, is increasing productivity through a strategy of growth with social justice and providing full employment to the rural sector within a ten year time frame. A comphrehensive strategy and approach for translating these objectives into specific programmes, the integrated rural development now contemplated involves a multi-pronged attack on the problem of rural development. 'Integrated' here covers four dimensions: Integration of sectoral programmes, spatial integration, integration of social and economic process and above all the policies with a view to achieve a balance between growth, removal of poverty and employment generation. More specifically, it involves a sharp focus on target groups comprising small and margional farmers, agricultural labourers and rural artisans, and extremely location-specific planning in rural areas".[12] As such, within the over-all strategy of development, the Sixth Five Year Plan categorically stated : "IRDP has been conceived essentially as an anti-poverty programme".[13]

During the five-year period (1980-85) in each block 600 poor families were to be assisted. In this way, a total of 15 million families below the poverty line were the target beneficiaries. The programme is implemented by a special administrative set up i.e. (DRDA's) District Rural Development Agencies in each district. The estimates show that, during Sixth Five Year Plan period, assets amounting to Rs. 50 billion were created and were distributed which benefitted about 17 million families. During 1987-88, the fourth year of the Seventh Plan another 4.2 million families were assisted with an investment of Rs. 4471 per family or Rs. 19 billion over-all.

There are numerous evaluations of IRDP-both by government departments and private researchers. In the past, most assessments by the government have been favourable,[14] but micro studies of IRDP have not been unequivocal in supporting the official claims. However, the divergence between macro indicators and micro-performance seem to be narrowing in recent years. Also, 'success' or 'failure' depend on the criterion adopted for assessment. Thus, Subba Rao (1985) argued that the most stringent criterion of crossing the 'poverty line' is inappropriate for judging the full benefits of this programme, since house-holds below the poverty line (poorest of the poor) may register incremental incomes and thus benefit from the programme, even if they are unable to cross the poverty income threshold.[15] Pulley [16] (1989) has shown that depending on the criterion adopted programme success rate varied. On the basis of criterion of "Investments remaining intact" (which suggests that house-holds are deriving incremental incomes from the asset), the programme is doing reasonably well even in relatively low income states like Bihar. But on the basis of the rigorous criterion of "crossing the poverty line", the success rate was very low. State-wise performance also suggests an inverse/interesting relationship between percentage of eligible beneficiaries and the proportion crossing the poverty line. Barring in the hill states (Himachal Pradesh and Jammu & Kashmir), the highest the proportion of eligible beneficiaries (i.e. lower the percentage of the non-poor) with low initial level of incomes, the more difficult it is for them to cross the poverty income threshold; the proportion doing so is small.[17]

The following Table 3.1 illustrates the measures of success of IRDP in major states.

Table -3.1
MEASURING OF SUCCESS OF IRDP

Major States	Percent Eligible * Beneficiaries	Percent Investment Intact **	Percent Eligible and Crossed Poverty Line***
1	2	3	4
A.P.	68	76	9
Arunachal Pradesh	73	61	4
Assam	27	70	10
Bihar	76	85	3
Gujarat	78	88	4
Haryana	71	46	0
Himachal Pradesh	87	85	29
J & K	97	80	19
Karnataka	85	64	4
Kerala	89	74	5
M.P.	81	73	6

1	2	3	4
Maharastra	83	69	10
Orissa	83	68	7
Punjab	30	77	18
Rajasthan	72	48	9
Tamil Nadu	83	63	3
U.P.	54	79	5
W.Bengal	46	97	8
Average	70	73	7

*   Proportion of Beneficiaries with pre-IRDP income < 4800

**   Proportion of IRDP Investments that remained fully operational after two years

*** Proportion of Beneficiaries with [.e-IRDP income < 4800 and Post-IRDP income = 6400 after two years in current price terms

Source : National Concurrent Evaluation of IRDP, Ministry of Rural Development, as quoted in Pulley (1989)

Bandyopadyaya (1988), expressed similar view regarding the evaluation of the impact of IRDP. He mentioned two important indices to reasonably assess the impact of the Programme: (i) whether the assisted families realised higher income than unassisted families; and (ii) whether the assisted families progressively climbed the next higher income bracket from the pre-investment income bracket.[18]

There are four major All-India Studies carried out by the National Bank of Rural Development (NABARD), Reserve Bank of India (RBI) the Programme Evaluation Organisation (PEO) of the Planning Commission and the Institute of Financial Management and Research (IFMR). Though these studies have their own limitations (i.e. studies relate only to the first two and a half years of the programme and their coverage has been rather small), can throw a light into the evaluatory literature on IRDP.[19]

The following 3.2 and 3.3 Tables illustrate some findings of the Evaluation Studies on IRDP and coverage of Evaluation of IRDP.

Table - 3.2

SOME FINDINGS OF THE EVALUATION STUDIES ON IRDP

	Percentage of Sample Households which crossed the Poverty Line	Percentage of Sample Households which received incremental income
IFMR	NR	84.2 *
RBI	17 **	51
NABARD	47	82
PEO	49.4	88

* were 'very happy' and 'happy' with IRDP

** Income of the Beneficiaries at current prices were discounted by 27 percent in order to arrive at their real income on March 1981 prices

NR: Not Reported

Source: Prepared from the Statistical Tables of all the four reports

Table - 3.3

COVERAGE OF EVALUATION OF IRDP

Coverage	IFMR	RBI	NABARD	PEO
Number of States	2	16	15	16
Number of Districts	5	16	30	33
Number of Blocks	17	16	60	66
Sample size	1859	730	1498	1170
Percentage of sample to the total beneficiary families	0.011	0.004	0.009	0.007

The most disappointing feature that came out of these studies is that the performance of the lowest income group of beneficiaries has been dismal. According to RBI, only 5 percent of the lowest fractile of the poor could cross the poverty line. According to PEO, the figure is 8.4 percent. Thus, the 'very poor' could not be fully taken care of under the IRDP. The main reasons for the failure of selected beneficiaries to cross the poverty line were :(i) very low pre-assistance income (ii) the incremental income through asset endowment was not sufficient to cover the gap because of insufficiency of investment per house-hold and (iii) lack of institutional or organisational support in the post-investment stage.

A recent study undertaken in Uttar Pradesh by Ch.Hanumanth Rao and others effectively refutes the criticism on IRDP that the programme is benefiting the house-holds closer to the poverty line, and the ultra-poor are unable to take advantage of the scheme. "In fact, in an administratively weak and relatively poor state like Uttar Pradesh, it has been found, based on panel data for 4 years, that the poorest house-holds not only managed to hold on to assets, but also found to be deriving income from the asset on a sustained basis".[20] The problem encountered by poorest house-holds was the continued reluctance of the institutional credit agencies to lend working capital on a regular basis even after the house-holds have proven their credit-worthiness by promptly repaying the IRDP loans. In other words, IRDP enabled access to institutional credit for the poorest house-holds as a one shot injection, but failed to open a channel of credit line on a continuing basis for the neediest house-holds not withstanding their proven credit-worthiness.[21]

Recent evidence suggests that wherever the investments choice of assets are properly dovetailed with the level and structure of demand in the region; the assets supplied were labour intensive in character, and supporting market net works were simultaneously promoted and wherever the programme reached the lower half of the poverty groups, its impact on the hardcore poor was substantial. However, for sustained income generation, it would be necessary to ensure continued access to institutional credit'for the poorest of the poor.[22]

3. NATIONAL RURAL EMPLOYMENT
PROGRAMME (NREP)

The National Rural Employment Programme (NREP) is a modified version of the food-for-work programme (only food grains were made available to the state governments under the FWP). However, the provision of cash component was introduced for the purchase of materials for the creation of durable productive assets under the NREP. The ratio between the value of food grains and cash grants to be given to the states is roughly 2:1. A total of Rs. 980 crores has been provided for the programme during the Sixth Plan period by the centre. The NREP is proposed to cover one thousand unemployed workers initially in each of the five thousand blocks in the country.

The programme has the following basic objectives ;

1. Generation of additional gainful employment for the unemployed and the under-employed persons, both men and women, in rural areas.

2. Creation of durable community assets for strengthening the rural infrastructure which will lead to rapid growth of rural economy and steady rise in the income levels of the rural poor.

3. Improvement in the nutritional levels of the rural poor. The programme is implemented through the State Governments and Union Territories in accordance with the guidelines prescribed by the Central Government.

The various kinds of works to be taken up under the NREP are:

1. Afforestation and social foresty.

2. Drinking water wells, community irrigation wells, group housing and land development projects for S.C. and S.Ts.

3. Construction and repairing of village tanks.

4. Minor irrigation works including drainage.

5. Soil and water conservation and land reclamation.

6. Rural roads.

7. School and Balwadi buildings, Panchayat ghars, Community centres, Cattle ponds, drinking water sources for the wild animals in the forest areas, community,

poultry and piggery houses, bathing and washing places, community toilets, community garbage pits and community bio-gas plants.

RURAL LANDLESS EMPLOYMENT GUARANTEE PROGRAMME

A Rural Landless Employment Guarantee Programme (RLEGP) was announced by the late Prime Minister Indira Gandhi on August 15, 1983 as a special programme to mitigate the suffering of the rural masses. It has been taken up as a centrally sponsored programme for which the entire expenditure is met by the Union Government.

The Government feels that the two programmes NREP and RLEGP should continue side by side until a decision on their merger is taken after watching their implementation. One view is that the centre should involve itself only in the new RLEGP and leave NREP to be funded by the State Governments themselves from the Seventh Plan onwards.

Pending a final decision, the Centre has asked the Planning Commission to allocate a massive amount of Rs. 500 crores for the RLEGP for 1984-85, the last year of the Sixth Five Year Plan. In the year 1983 Rs. 100 crores was provided for the programme.

The RLEGP guarantees employment to atleast one member of every landless labour household upto 100 days in an year and aims at creating durable assests for strengthening the rural infrastructure, leading to rapid growth of rural economy. In the year 1983 about 300 million mandays were to be generated.

EVALUATION OF NREP AND RLEGP

The combined employment generation under the two wage-employment programmes, viz, NREP and RLEGP works out to around 700 million mandays per year. The annual out-lay for this order of employment generation is roughly about Rs. 1500 crores per annum. However, current estimates reveal that, about 450 million mandays of employment per annum was generated under these two programmes up to the year 1988.

Here, again evaluations pointed out that: (i) the impact of the programmes on the total income of poor house-holds was insignificant, because they met only about 9 percent of the demand for work from the poor in rural areas: (ii) the programmes could not create sufficiently useful wage intensive works at times and in places most needed; (iii) the poor couldn't benefit from the assets created; (iv) the assets created were of poor quality and (v) wages actually paid were lower than budgeted owing to leakage and corruption. The above criticism may not be authentic one in two. A recent estimate by Subba Rao suggests that NREP provided nearly 40 percent of the total incremental employment in rural India.[23] A major problem in studying the impact of NREP and RLEGP is the absence of any All-India evaluation scheme. The annual Report, 1986-87 of the Ministry of Rural Development listed some of the deficiencies in NREP programme: (a) employment being provided under the programme is for short durations; (b) planning of the works and co-ordination with different departments was found grossly inadequate; and (c) selection of beneficiaries was not proper in as much as the poorest, for whom the programme is meant were often left out and there were no maintenance of the assets created under the programme. The only systematic study on NREP, on which some reliance can be placed is that of Indira Hirway.[24] According to Hirway there are three factors which were jointly responsible for the blemishes observed in NREP. These are:

    (i) inept design of the programme itself.

    (ii) constraints of the administration and

    (iii) imbecile administration.

The RLEG Programme also suffers from functional weaknesses. The study made by the Punjab Institute of Public Administration reveals that only 5 percent of the workers had worked for 100 days or more, though 82 percent were from the families identified as below the poverty line. An ILO [25] report indicates from a sample survey, that the average employment provided for a person was 51 days and 55 days in Gujrat and Karnataka respectively and NREP employment contributed around 24 percent of the total income of the sample house-hold. Thus, "the long term goal of the employment programme, namely, the rehabilitation of the poor in the main stream of the economy by increasing its labour absorbing capacity through the creation of durable and productive assets, does not seem to be capable of attainment under NREP/RLEGP as being presently implemented.[26]

JAWAHAR ROJGAR YOJANA (JRY)

The importance of employment programme in reducing rural poverty is also reflected in the Seventh Five Year Plan (1985-90) which emphasises food work and productivity; and aims at providing productive employment to every one seeking it and assigning priority to activities which contribute most effectively to this purpose. In the year 1989-90 a new scheme named as (JRY) Jawahar Rojgar Yojana[27] by merging NREP and RLEGP, to provide employment opportunities has been launched. The expenditure under this programme is to be shared between the centre and states on 80:20 basis. The central assistance under this programme is to be released to the district directly. No less than 80 percent of allocations under the programme received by the district are required to be given to the village panchayats. It is estimated that the new programme provides fuller employment opportunities to atleast one member of each family living below the poverty line, who seeks unskilled employment. It is also hoped that distribution of resources to village panchayats will result in increasing the coverage of the programme to all the rural areas.

OBJECTIVES OF JAWAHAR ROJGAR YOJANA

Primary Objectives: Generation of additional gainful employment for the unemployed and under employed persons both men and women in the rural areas.

Secondary Objectives: (I) Creation of Productive assets for direct and continuing benefits to the poverty groups and for strengthening rural, economic and social infrastructure, which will lead to rapid growth of rural economy and steady rise in the income level of the rural poor (ii) improvement in the overall qualities of life in the rural areas.

As the Jawahar Rojgar Yojana has been introduced in 1989, the evaluatory study is not yet available, but we hope, that this programme may achieve fruitful results owing to decentralisation of activity and active involvement of Gram Panchayats in the implementation.

The review of the special programmes, that are introduced to alleviate poverty and to generate employment in rural areas, reveals that except IRDP the other programmes have not achieved the desired results. Even the IRDP has not made a significant dent in the rural areas in accruing benefits to ultra-poor due to various limitations. The creation of productive assets and community infrastructure, which is the basic objective of these programmes has not been realised. Further more, these programmes were not integrated with the overall planning of the economy. Though the IRDP was aimed to be the integral part at the block level planning to involve the people in the gross-root level, to strengthen this programme and to achieve targeted results effectively has been neglected in due course of time on one or the other pretention.

IMPACT OF POVERTY-ERADICATION PROGRAMMES IN ANDHRA PRADESH

Since the mid 1970's various state governments have launched specific anti-poverty programmes along with implementing centrally sponsored poverty alleviation programmes. For example, Maharashtra's Employment Guarantee Scheme (MEGS), public distribution system and integrated Nutritional programmes were initiated by Tamil Naidu, Karnataka, Kerala and Andhra Pradesh (Rs. 2-a-kilo rice scheme).

In implementing Central Government programmes like IRDP, NREP, RLEGP AND now Jawahar Rojgar Yojana, Andhra Pradesh is in fore front. Recent estimates indicate that 2,29,984 persons in 1983-84 and 2,70,289 persons in 1984-85 were benefited under the Integrated Rural Development Programme (IRDP) similarly, the rural labour was provided employment for 228.99 lakh mandays in 1983-84 and 281.05 lakh mandays in 1984-85 under National Rural Employment Programme, and under (RLEGP) Rural Landless Employment Guarantee Programme 199. lakh mandays employment was provided in 1984-85. Under NREP, after Tamil Nadu, Andhra Pradesh have successfully attracted more women. Of the total employment of 34 million mandays, 48 percent were created involving women.

Andhra Pradesh is the only state which has taken up a unique housing programme during the year 1983-84. Under various schemes spending Rs.6000 to 10,000 per unit in rural areas up to 1988-89 nearly 7 lakh houses were constructed to provide shelter to the under-previleged economically backward and weaker sections of the society. Besides this, 3,77,469 house sites in 1983-84 and 3,24,567 in 1984-85 were alloted to the weaker sections.

Under Jawahar Rojgar Yojana, of the target of 772.78 lakh mandays set for the year 1990-91 up to March, 1990, 777.15 (100.56 percent) lakh mandays were created in Andhra Pradesh.

The impact of anti-poverty programme in Warangal district can be summarised as follows: Under IRDP of the target of 9809 persons to be benifited for the year 1990-91, the achievement up to March 1990 was estimated as 10,805 (110.15 percent). Under Jawahar Rojgar Yojana, of the target of 39.65 lakh mandays the achievement up to March 1990 was 43.95 lakh mandays (110.84 percent).

REFERENCES

1. Bandopadhyaya : Direct intervention programmes for poverty alleviation, EPW, June 25,1988 P.A.79.

2. Planning Commission : Approach to the Fifth Plan. (1974-79) January 1973,p.5

3. Planning Commission : Ibid p.9.

4. Hanumanth Rao C.H : Planning for poverty removal, Mainstream (weekly) edited by Nikhil Chakravarthy, New Delhi, 1984 p.14.

5. Bandopadhyaya : op-cit. p.79.

6. Planning Commission : Approach to Seventh Five Year Plan (1985- 90) Vol. 2 p.61.

7. Ibid : p.62.

8. Kamat Prasad : Planning for Poverty Alleviation, Agricole Publishing Academy, 1985, p.38.

9. Kamat Prasad : Ibid. p.39.

10. Govt. of India : Fifth Five Year Plan p.p.233-234.

11. Planning Commission: Sixth Five Year Plan p.172.

12. Planning Commission: Draft Sixth Five Year Plan (1978-83)

13. Planning Commission: Sixth Five Year Plan(1980-85) Mid term appraisal, 1983.

14. Kakwani N and
    Subba Rao K   :   Rural poverty and its alleviation in India, EPW Vol.. xxiv No.32 March 31, 1990 P.A-12.

15. Subba Rao. K   :   Regional variations in impact of anti-poverty programmes, EPW Oct.26, 1985.

16. Kakwani N and
    Subba Rao K   :   op-cit P.A.12

17. Pulley.V   :   Making the poor credit worthy, World Bank Discussion paper No.58.

18. Bandhyopodyay. D   :   op-cit P.A.-81

19. Bandhyopodyay. D   :   op-cit PA 80

20. Hanmanth Rao, CH :   Efficiency of investments in IRDP: A & Ranga Swamy P : Study of Uttar Pradesh, EPW, June 25,1988.

21. Kakwani, N and
    Subba Rao, K   op-cit P.A.-12

22. Subba Rao, K   :   Regional variation in impact of anti-poverty programmes, E.P.W. Oct.26,1985.

23. Subba Rao,K   :   Ibid

24. Indira Hirway   :   Special employment programmes on rural development: A study of NREP in Gujarat, Mimeo, Sardar Patel Institute of Economic and Social Research, Ahmedabad, 1984.

25. ILO   :   Summary results of the socio-economic survey on sample projects of the NREP, Geneva, Jan.1984, quoted in Bugchi's article in EPW, Jan.24,1987.

26. Bugchi, Sandeep   :   Poverty alleviation programme in Seventh Plan: An appraisal, EPW, Jan.24, 1987.

27. Government of India,
    Ministry of
    Agriculture   :   Mannual of Rural Development, Jawahar Rojgar Yojana, New-Delhi, 1989.

4

PROBLEM SETTING AND METHODOLOGY

The rural economy of India once self-sufficient prior to the British era has not yet gained the same prestigious position even after decades of planning. Though, the intensity of the problems might have changed a bit, but the basic issues are still lingering around.

PROBLEM SETTING

The dual exploitation by semi feudal exploitative class of rural sector and the capitalist class of the urban sector are causing unbearable sufferings to the landless labourers, marginal farmers, small peasants and even middle class peasants. At the bottom of rural structure are the landless labourers class who generally constitute a large proportion of the agricultural population. People belonging to this class are the poorest of the poor. They have neither security of employment nor the income. They normally find some work during the sowing and harvesting seasons, except that, they are virtually unemployed during the rest of the year.

Though various state governments have enacted legislation for the introduction of minimum wages, such Legislation is rarely enforced rigorously in a rural society which is dominated by vested interests. The wages that the landless labourers actually receive are generally at the level of bare subsistence. They are perpetually in a state of indebtedness to the rich farmers who also act as money lenders. This is caused basically by eternal poverty but aggravated due to social obligations and expenditure on religious and social ceremonies and rituals. The spread of banking sector to the rural areas in recent decades has not changed their position significantly. A considerable proportion of the landless labourers have been forced by this state of affairs to become bonded labourers. various state governments taking[1] steps to eradicate this socio economic evil has not been, so effective.

Slightly, above the landless labourers class in economic status or the millions of small and marginal farmers who generally own little land, which, however is almost never adequate even for a bare subsistence.[2] The families of these small and marginal farmers with inadequate and uneconomic holdings represent most of the disguised unemployment in the rural sector. Some members of these families generally offer themselves whole time or part-time laboureres during agricultural season. this section of peasants also can be visualised as a formidable group of tenants. Other things being equal tenants income will be even lower than those of small operator owners, and the amount of the land required for an income above the poverty line is correspondingly larger.[3]

In an economic condition, roughly comparable to that of the small and marginal peasants are the village artisans and craftsmen including blacksmiths, cobblers, potters, weavers, fishermen, carpenters, small shop keepers. Though self-employed, this class generally shares the poverty of the lower economic strata of the peasantry, and is unable to rise above the poverty the lacking in capital and modern technology, operating on a very low scale of production, and catering to a very limited market, this class represents more of legacy of the past than of promise for the future.[4]

The so-called land reforms, green revolution, Banks nationalisation and the host of other welfare programmes have not changed rural situation in any significant way. Inspite of limit ed growth of capitalism in agricultural sector, the land rela tions remain essentially pre-capitalistic. The influence of money lenders still exist. Mode of production, market structure, price dichotomy between industrial goods and agricultural goods and weak bargaining and organisational power still holds in the rural economy.

The agricultural labourers, small and marginal farmers, rural artisans and other service rendering classes of the rural structure are the major chunk that is exposed to abject poverty. Most of them are deprived of even basic needs and suffer from mal-nutrition, poor housing, health and educational facilities, which in turn is the cause for their low level of efficiency.

Ragnar Nurkse[5] popularised the 'vicious circle of poverty' in early 1950s which had been formulate earlier by Gunnar Myrdal with reference to poverty of the Negroes in U.S.A.[6] Nurkse asserts that poverty breeds poverty in a chain of circular causation and formulated as follow: it employs, of course, a circular constellation of forces tending to act and react upon one another in such a way as to keep a poor country in a state of poverty. For example, a poor man may be weak; being physically weak, his working capacity may be low which means that he is poor, which in turn means that he will not have enough to eat; and so on. A situation of this sort, relating to a country as whole, can be summed up in trite proposition: ' a country is poor because it is poor.'[7] Gunnar Myrdal has rightly pointed out, if Nurkse's poor man produced less food than would enable him to survive in a state of health necessary for maintaining barely the existing level of production, he would in fact gradually become poorer because he is poor.[8]

J.K. Galbraith, while sharing the views on the vicious circle theory, recently suggested modifications which would make it even more pessimistic than its original formulations.[9] Galbraith argues that even if the equilibrium of mass poverty in poor countries, which is a predominantly rural phenomenon, is broken, it would tend to restore itself. If the income of the community rises, for instance, due to new-technology or new investments, this would lead to additional consumption rather than additional investment, partly because of the intensity of poverty and partly because of population growth. Low saving and investment, added work force due to population explosion would result in a progressively lower yield in turn restores low levels of equilibrium. Hence, Galbraith argues that " There are built into the structure of poverty, the social and biological forces by which improvement is aborted, the poverty perpetuated".[10] He further argues that the will to break out of the vicious circle of poverty is generally replaced by the spirit of accommodation and co-existence with it, since the vast rural masses have witnessed the futile attempts that have been made to break it in the light of their age-old experience.

The major aspect in eradication of poverty lies with a well conceived understanding of the problem of poverty. In this regard, the discussion boils down to three sets of explanations for the existence of poverty and its perpetuation. In ancient times poverty was generally explained in terms of sin. The doctrine of KARMA which still exists in a predominantly religious and traditional country like India, basically insists on Karma or fate as the source of poverty. The personal misdeeds of individuals in past and present life being are attributed to their present position. People believe in the Hindu Maxim: "Action is the duty, result is not thy concern". This approach obviously places the source of poverty outside the soci-economic structure of the society. "As a sequel of the complacent attitude of the Indians, the old systems of production and distribution got perpetuated".[11]

According to the other explanation factors such as over population, relatively poor natural resources, illiteracy, backward technology and low level of productivity etc are the source of poverty.[12] Some other extended the gamut of causes of poverty to cover, inter-alia, foreign rule, exploitation of masses and social attitudes.[13]

The third school of thought totally differs from the other two and maintains that poverty is an out come of social and economic inequalities in the society[14], and it is due to exploitation of man by man that largely accounts for the staggering dimensions of poverty.[15]

The scientific outlook towards the genesis of poverty throws light into the above discussion, and compels us to think on constructive lines that is, poverty is the result of concentration of productive resources in few hands and various forms of exploitation existing in the society. We should not ignore the closely inter-linked global and National structures of dominance and exploitation, while understanding the problem of poverty.

Various economists, social scientists and governmental agencies are measuring the extent of poverty both in rural and urban areas time to time, by adopting various methods. Most of the studies have taken calorie as the basis of constructing the per capita consumption expenditure line (poverty line) to measure the poverty. Dandekar and Rath justified their study on calorie intake base by stating that "The non-food items are more important in the consumer expenditure of the rich rather than the poor".[16] But in recent times calorie intake approach has been subjected to major criticism. This approach suffers from major weakness i.e. it ignores the consumption expenditure on non-food items which is becoming stable part in the consumption pattern of the poor.

It is the time now to develop new yard-sticks for measuring poverty which would recognise the multiple manifestations of its incidence, and not merely the lack of purchasing power of food items. Recently, the planning commission has set up a panel of experts for reviewing and improving upon the methodology for determining the poverty ratio. A composite index of poverty has to be evolved which encompasses the major areas of deprivation that poverty represents such as food, clothing, housing, water supply and sanitation, education and health.

It is under this premise and with the above mentioned broad objectives that the present study has been undertaken. The following section presents the methodology adopted in the empirical study.

METHODOLOGY

The methodology adopted in this study, and the profile of the sample villages are discussed in this section.

OBJECTIVES OF THE STUDY

The main objectives of the present study are as follows:

1. To provide a historical perspective of the genesis of poverty, in general, and rural poverty, in particular.
2. To present an overview of the existing studies on poverty in India and make a review of the trends in rural poverty on the basis of the earlier studies.
3. To examine the socio-economic dimensions of rural poverty of the sample house-holds in the study area with reference to the levels of consumption expenditure.
4. To analyse the spatial aspects of rural poverty.
5. To examine the efficacy of the various anti-poverty programmes initiated by the Government.

RESEARCH DESIGN

The position of the respondents with respect to the poverty line has been estimated on the basis of per capita monthly consumption expenditure of the respondents. The poverty line defined by the Seventh Five Year Plan has been adopted in this study.

In Seventh Five Year Plan, the criterion of the poverty is linked to calorie intake of 2400 per person per day in rural areas and of 2100 in urban areas, the cut-off point for measuring poverty is per capita monthly consumer expenditure of Rs. 107 and 122 respectively, for rural and urban areas at 1984-85 prices.

A field study has been conducted in 9 villages, 3 from each Mandal in Warangal district. Shayampet, Pathipaka, Taherpur of

Shayampet Mandal, Laxmidevipet, Ramanujapur, Peddapur of Venkatpaur Mandal and Narmetta, Veldandi and Ammapur of Narmetta Mandal are selected for the purpose of present study. The total sample size in study villages is 300 respondents. 100 respondents each from three Mandals.

DATA BASE AND DATA COLLECTION TOOLS

The data used for this study mainly come from primary source through structured questionnaire. To acquire adequate information, interview method is also adopted. Data regarding soci-economic profile of the sample villages, family structure, land ownership, working and consumption patterns and particulars related to productive assets, house-hold assets and migration data were collected by canvassing a questionnaire among respond ents. In order to have some standardisation in measuring the consumption expenditures, the retail prices as reported by the village retail shop keepers, are averaged and used in the valuation of physical quantities consumed. Such standardised prices are also used for estimating the money value asset.

Consumption expenditure level related to Andhra Pradesh has been collected from data published by Bureau of Economics and Statistics, Hyderabad. Information related to functioning of anti-poverty programmes in Andhra Pradesh and in Warangal district has been gathered from report prepared by the Finance and Planning Departments, Government of Andhra Pradesh and District Rural Development Agency and Chief Planning Officer of Warangal district respectively.

Analytical tools used to process and analyse the data include bivariate, multi-variate tables and bar diagrams. Tools used for processing the data includes simple frequency counts, percentages and averages.

SAMPLE DESIGN

As mentioned earlier, the field study has been undertaken in 9 villages spread over 3 Mandals viz Shayampet, Venkatapur and Narmetta in Warangal district. The selection has been made on the basis of different geographical features of the Mandals viz Venkatapur Mandal is a relatively well irrigated area, Narmetta is a drought prone region and the geographical feature of the Shayampet Mandal is a unique one. It is neither well irrigated area nor completely dry area. A modest attempt has been made to study the levels of living in these three Mandals which have divergent geographical, climatic, demographic and socio-economic conditions.

PRELIMINARY SURVEY AND PRE-TESTING

Prior to the actual field study, a preliminary survey was conducted in one of the sample villages, Shayampet and a pretesting is made on the variables to be included and the possible response from the respondents. A decision to include the variables in the questionnaire has been made only after conducting preliminary survey and pre-testing.

In this section the profile of the study district Warangal, the profile of the selected Mandals i.e Shayampet, Venkatapur and Narmetta, and the profile of the sample villages i.e. Shayampet, Pathipaka, Taherpur, Laxmidevipet, Peddapur, Ramanujpur, Narmetta, Veldandi and Ammapur has been discussed.

PROFILE OF WARANGAL DISTRICT

Warangal District lies between the Latitude of 17-19 and 18-36' North and Longitude of 78-49 and 80-43 East. It is bounded on the North by Karimnagar District. On the West by Medak District, on the south by Nalgonda District and by Khammam District is 12846 Sq. K.Ms. for the purpose of administration the District was divided in to three Revenue Divisions and 50 Revenue Mandals. The soils of the District comprise of sandy Loams with patches of shallow Block cotton soils. As the district is situated at considerable distance from the sea coast, its climate generally tends to be dry and there is no much fluctuation in the temperature. It gets quite warm during the summer months also continues to be warm in the rest of the year except during the December and January, when the temperature drops slightly. The mean daily Maximum & Minimum temperature have been recorded as 42.9 and 16.2 in '0' Centigrade respectively.

The rainy season sets in the District with the on set of South-West monsoon in the later part of the June month, and ends with the month of September with the closure of the South-West monsoon. The normal annual rainfall of the District is 987.3 m.m. The maximum rainfall occurs in the months of July, August, September and the highest rainfall is received by Mulug, Parkal, Mahabubad and Narsampet Mandals.

The important irrigation sources in the District are Ramappa, Pakhal and Laknavaram and Salivagu project under which considerable area is irrigated. The other sources of irrigation in the District are rainfed tanks, wells and hill-streams which require good showers in the season.

There are 6 medium irrigation sources in the district with registered ayacut of 40,169.00 acres, of which one viz, Mallur vagu project is an on-going scheme.

DATA BASE AND DATA COLLECTION TOOLS

Out of the total cropped area of 12,41,691.00 acres, the area under food crops was 8,98,815 i.e. 72.4 percent and the area under non-food crops was 3,42,876 i.e. 27.6 percent (1986-87), the principal cereal crops grown in the district are rice, jowar and maize. Rice occupies first place in out-turn while Jowar occupies the first place in the area. In it's production of rice the district occupies 4th place in Telangana region and 11th place in Andhra Pradesh. According to the consumption of food grains the population of the district can be divided into fifty fifty in respect of rice eaters and millet eaters.

With a total population of 23.00 lakhs (1981 census) the District occupies 12th place in the State of A.P. The growth rate of population of the district during the decennial ending 1981 over 1971 was 23.01 percent as against 23.19 percent growth rate of the State. The total population of S.T.s and S.Cs in the district was 2.93 lakhs (12.60 percent) and 3.84 lakhs (16.7 percent) respectively. There are 179 persons per sq.km. in the district as against 195 in the State, and 17.2 percent of its population is living in urban area. The percentage of literacy in the district is 23.5 as against the State figures 29.9 percent. Only 13.6 percent of the female population of the district is literate as against the 20.4 percent of the State.

Out of 1098 villages of the district 1004 villages are inhabitated and the rest of the villages are deserted. The total rural population of the district is 19.04 lakhs. There are (4) Towns in the district viz: Warangal, Janagoan, Mahabubabad and Dornakal. The total urban population is 3.96 lakhs. warangal is classified as class I city with a rank of commissioner of muncipality. The working class population in the district is 9.86 lakhs which is 42.87 percent of the total population. The workers in agricultural sector are 7.15 lakhs forming 31.06 percent of the total population. The remaining 2.71 lakhs are the workers engaged in non-agricultural sectors comprising of 11.81 percent of the total population of the District. The non workers class population is 13.14 lakhs constituting 57.13 percent of the total population.

PROFILE OF THE SELECTED MANDALS

SHAYAMPET MANDAL

The Shayampet Mandal came into existence in May 1985 by carving out 12 villages from erstwhile Parkal taluka. It is bounded on the north by Parkal, on the south by Atmakur on the east by Atmakur and Regonda and west by parkal Mandals. Its geographical area is 121 Sq.Kms. This Mandal gets rainfall from south west monsoon. The maximum and minimum temperatures in this Mandal is at 45-5 and 28-6 respectively. The average rainfall recorded in 1984-85 was 1096.1 mm. The population is 34,400 (as per 1981 census) and the density of population was estimated as 314 per sons per sq.km. of the total population 19.0 percent are of sheduled caste and 2.4 percent sheduled tribes. Out of the total working population of 15,360. 26 percent are cultivators, 46 percent are agricultural laboureres and the remianing 28 percent are non-agricultural workers. 18.5 percent of the total popula tion are literates, of these 83 percent are male literates. Of the total land available for cultivation 79 percent land is under active cultivation. This Mandal predominately contains balck soils and red chalka soils. The gross irrigated area is 11,606 acres. The important irrigation source in this Mandal is chaliva gu, the ayacut under this project is 3046 acres. The other source of irrigation is from Tanks and Small Ponds.

There are 4 secondary schools, 5 upper primary schools and 22 primary schools in this Mandal. There is only one primary health centre, one Ayurvedic hospital and a commercial Bank Branch. These two are situated in the Mandal head quarter (shayampet).

VENKATAPUR MANDAL

Venkatapur Mandal also came into existence from May 1985 with 10 villages. All the 10 villages belonged to erstwhile Mulug taluq. To the north Bhoopalpally Mandal, Mulug and govindaraopet Mandal to the south, Tadwai Mandal to the east and to the west Mulug, Ghanpur and Regonda Mandal situated as boundaries to the Venkatapur Mandal. Its geographical area is 246 Sq. Kms, and it gets its rainfall from south-west monsoons. The maximum and minimum temperatures generally lies around 45-5 and 28-6 respectively. The average rainfall in this Mandal is 1039.m.m. The population as per 1981 census worked out as 30.104 of which 15,211 (50.52%) are male population and 14,893 (49.48%) are the female population. The density of population was 122 persons per Sq.Km of the total population 16 percent belonged to scheduled caste and 12 percent scheduled tribes. Of the total working population of 14,521,25 percent are cultivators 53 percent are agricultural labourers and the remaining 22 percent are non- agricultural workers. 17.3 percent of the population are literates, of these 76 percent are male literates.

Of the total cultivable land in this Mandal 65 percent is under actual cultivation. Most of the soils are black and sandy. The gross irrigation area in this Mandal is 14,606 acres. The most significant source of irrigation is Ramappa lake with an ayacut of 6000 acres. The other important source of irrigation comes from tanks and ponds.

There are 2 secondary schools, 8 upper primary schools and 28 primary schools in this Mandal. There is one primary health centre and one homeopathy hospital. Two branches of Kakatiya Grameena Bank, one in Mandal head quarter and the other in Narsapur village are situated.

The Ramappa temple located in Palampet village of this Mandal is a historically highly sculptured temple built by the Ganapathi Deva of Kakatiya dynasty. This piligrimage centre is attracting histroians and archealogists.

NARMETTA MANDAL

The Narmetta Mandal too came into existence in May 1985 by carving out 16 villages from erstwhile Cheriyala taluk. To its north is Kareemnagar district, south Jangoan and Raghunathpally Mandals, to the east Ghanpur Mandal and to the west Maddur and Bachannapet Mandals.

The geographical area of this Mandal is 219.7 Sq.Km. This mandal too gets rainfall from south-west mansoons, but it is often a drought hit area. The average rainfall is only 764.8 m.m. The population in this Mandal according to 1981 census was 31,599 and the density of the population was 137 persons per Sq.Km. of the total population 19 percent are scheduled caste and 16 percent are scheduled tribes. Of the total working population of 15865, 53 percent are cultivators, 32 percent agricultural labourers and the remaining 15 percent are of non-agricultural workers. 16.9 percent of the total population are litcrates, of these 75 percent are male literates.

60 percent of the total cultivable land is under active cultivation. Most of the lands are of red and sandy soils. Only small ponds and tanks are the source of water to the limited acreage. The 99 percent of irrigated area depends on under ground water resource only.

There are 2 secondary schools, 2 upper primary schools and 20 primary schools in this mandal. There is one primary health centre at the Mandal head quarter. A branch of District Co- operative bank and Bank of Baroda are situated at Narmetta i.e. the mandal head quarter. A branch of Kakatiya Grameena Bank working at Tarigoppula village.

PROFILE OF THE SAMPLE VILLAGES OF DIFFERENT MANDALS

The following paragraphs are devoted to depict the profiles of the sample villages selected for this study viz Shayampet, Pathipaka, Taherpur of Shayampet Mandal, Laxmidevipet, Peddapur, Ramanujapur of Venkatapur Mandal and Narmetta, Veldandi and Ammapur of Narmetta Mandal.

SHAYAMPET MANDAL

Shayampet village is situates at a distance of 24 Km away from district head quarter Warangal, with a total area of 1065.13 Sq.Km. having a population of 5632 of which 51.99 percent are male population 48.01 percent female population. Only 29.83 of the population are literates. Of the total population 31.28 percent are working. The village has no major irrigation source and mostly depends on small tanks. Only 36.07 percent of total cultivated area is under irrigation. This village is predominantly having rural artisans (65 percent are weavers) and other workers who are mostly engaged in Beedi making. As this village in the mandal head quarter, it is having one primary health centre, one commercial Bank (SBI Branch) and a market yard. 2 handloom weavers-cooperative societies and one Agricul tural Co-operative society are functioning.

The Pathipaka village situated at about 26 Kms away from Warangal with an area of 985.Sq.Kms is having a population of 3206 of which 51.34 percent male population and the remaining 48.66 percent are female. This village has only 17.15 percentage of literates. The total working population works out to 1714 of the total population. Of the total land under assured irrigation. This village has neither proper medical nor educational facility.

The Taherpur which is also 21 Kms away from Warangal with an area of 678.25 Sq. Kms. is having population of 1785 of which 4969 are male and 50.31 percent are female population. Here also the literacy rate is very low, of the total population 19.49 percent are literates.

The working population in this village is 48.91 percent of the total population. This village is predominantly getting irrigation from wells. Of the total area under cultivation 52.72 percent is having irrigation facility.

Agriculture is the main occupation in these 3 villages. Of these only Taherpur has irrigation facility at greater length. The highest literacy in the sample villages is in shayampet. Here the percentage of literates 29.83, where as the literacy in Taherpur and Pathipaka are 19.49 and 17.15 percent respectively.

VENKATPUR MANDAL

Laxmidevipet in Venkatpur Mandal has an area of 2547.09 Sq.Kms and population of 4797 of which 50.99 percent are of male and 49.01 percentage female population. The literacy rate is 15.92 percent which is second to the literacy rate in Ramanujpur of 21.05 percent of total population. The literacy rate in Peddapur village is lowest at 11.25 percent. Peddapur is 42 Kms away from Warangal, and having an area 3260.95 Sq.Kms with population of 3802 of which 50.24 percent are male population. Ramanujapur with an area of 2453.60 Sq.Kms is having a population 2774 of this 51.87 percent are male population. The working population is lowest with 41.47 percent in Peddapur village, the highest is in the RAmanujapur (51.65 percent). Laxmidevipet occupying the middle position with 48.57 percent of working population. This mandal is having highest irrigation potential than other mandals. Ramappa lake with an ayacut of 6000 acres is situated in this mandal. Hence, the Ramanujapur which is getting maximum benefit from this source is having an irrigation potential of 80.34 percent of the total cultivated area. Peddapur occupies second position with 58.73 percent and Laxmidevipet with 54.0 percent is in the third position.

NARMETTA MANDAL

Narmetta village, which is also the Mandal head Quarter is 66 Kms away from the district headquarter Warangal, is having a population of 5955, of which 50.49 percent are male population. Veldandi, with a population of 3867 of which 49.98 percent are male population is 64 Kms away from Warangal. The other village Ammapur, which is 70 Kms away from Warangal, with an area of 940.89 Sq. Kms is having 1957 population. 977 persons (49.92) are male population and 50.08 are female. The literacy rate is highest in Ammapur (25.65 percent), followed by Veldandi and Narmetta with 22.29 and 18.29 percent respectively. The working population is highest in Veldandi (57.33 percent) followed by 44.51 and 43.02 in Narmetta and Ammapur villages respectively. The irrigation facility available is highest in Ammapur with 51.92 percent followed by 27.26 in Veldandi and 24.14 in Narmetta.

Being the Mandal head quarter one primary health centre, one branch each of District Co-operative Bank and Bank of Baroda are situated in this village only.

REFERENCES

1. Government of India : Report of the commissioner for (S.C. and STs 27th Report) 1977-81, controller of publications 1983, p.p. 26-35.

2. : World Bank, Rural Development, op-cit; p.23

3. Ibid : p.23

4. Bandopadhyaya J : The Poverty of Nations, a global perspective of Mass Poverty in the third world, Allied Publishers, Ahmedabad, 1988, 1.17.

5. Ragnar Nurkse : Problems of capital Formations in under developed countries, Oxford, 1953, p.4

6. Gunnar Myrdal : An American Dilemma:The Negro problem and modern democracy, Harper and Brothers, New York, 1944, chapter III section 7

7. Ragnar Nurkse : op-cit, p.4

8. Gunnar Myrdal : Asian Drama, vol III, penguin press London p.p.184-185

9. Bandopadhyay : op-cit, p.241

10. Galbraith J.K : The Nature of Masses Poverty, Harward University Press, Cambridge, Mass: 1979 p.56-59

11. Dwivedi D.N   :   Economic concentration and poverty,
                             Harward University Press, Cambridge,
                             Mass; 1979 p.p.56-59

12. Gunnar Myrdal   :   "The challenge of World Poverty
                             penguin press, 1970,pp.30.45

13. Dwivedi D.N   :   op-cit, p.15

14. Sen A.K   :   Poverty,   Inequality   and
                             Unemployment: Some conceptual
                             issues in measurements, EPW Vol.
                             XVIII No. 31-33, 1973,p.1457

15. Ranjith Sen   :   'On Rural Poverty', A tentative
                             hypothesis, EPW Vol. XVIII No.
                             56,1973, p.2564

16. Dandekar and Rath   :   op-cit, p.29

5

PATTERNS OF RURAL POVERTY: A CASE STUDY OF WARANGAL DISTRICT

The present project is empirical study conducted in 9 villages of Warangal district, for estimating the extent of rural poverty and understanding it's socio-economic dimensions. This chapter examines the results of the empirical study.

The socio-economic background and other particulars of the sample respondents are presented in the following section.

CATEGORY-WISE DISTRIBUTION OF THE SAMPLE RESPONDENTS

Table 5.1 shows the category-wise distribution of the sample units. Out of 300 respondents selected for the sample, 78 each belong to marginal farmers, rural artisans and agricultural labourers categories. The remaining 66 respondents are from other categories of rural servants such as cobblers, barbers, washermen and others. In each Mandal 100 respondents were selected. Of these 26 each are marginal farmers, rural artisans and agricultural labourers and 22 respondents from each Mandal are from 'others' category.

Out of 9 villages selected for the study from the 3 Mandals, 3 big villages i.e Shayampet, Laxmidevipet and Narmetta were identified and ten respondents from each category were selected from these villages. In the remaining six villages, 8 respondents from marginal farmers, rural artisans and agricultural labourers were picked up. Six more respondents are selected from others category in each village.

Table -5.1

CATEGORY-WISE DISTRIBUTION OF SAMPLE HOUSE-HOLDS SELECTED
MANDALS

Name of Mandal	M.F.	R.A.	A.L.	Other	Total
I. Shayampet	26	26	26	22	100
II. Venkatapur	26	26	26	22	100
III. Narmetta	26	26	26	22	100
Total	78	78	78	66	300

Source: Field Data

COMMUNITY-WISE DISTRIBUTION OF SAMPLE RESPONDENTS

The community-wise distribution of sample respondents is as shown in Table 5.2. Of the total 300 respondents chosen for study, 55 come from Scheduled Caste Communities, 27 from Scheduled Tribes, 159 from Backward Class Communities and 59 from other communities. While the number of S.C.respondents is the highest in Narmetta Mandal, S.Ts outnumber other communities in Venkatapur Mandal. Further B.C. respondents are more than other categories respondents in Shayampet Mandal. This is conforms to the population trends in the three Mandals.

Thus, the community composition of the sample is so designed to be in conformity.

AGE-WISE DISTRIBUTION OF SAMPLE RESPONDENTS

As is evident from the figures presented in Table 5.3, out of the total 300 respondents selected from 9 villages 78 (26.0 percent) are between 31-40 years, 87 (29.0 percent) are between 41-50 years, 16 (5.33 percent) are between 51-60 years and 4 (1.33 percent) respondents are above 60 years of age. Highest number of respondents

are in the age group of 31-40 years followed by 41- 50, 20-30, 51-60 and
61 and above age groups.

Table- 5.2

COMMUNITY-WISE DISTRIBUTION OF SAMPLE RESPONDENTS

S.No.	Name of the village with Mandal	S.C.	S.T.	B.C.	O.C.	Total
I. SHAYAMPET MANDAL						
1. Shayampet		7	1	26	6	40
2. Pathipaka		5	1	16	8	30
3. Taherpur		3	1	18	8	30
II. VENKATAPUR						
4. Laxmidevipet		7	10	18	5	40
5. Peddapur		3	5	15	7	30
6. Ramanujapur		6	3	13	8	30
III. NARMETTA						
7. Narmetta		7	3	24	6	40
8. Veldandi		6	3	16	5	30
9. Ammapur		11	-	13	6	30
Total		55	27	159	59	300
		(18.33)	(9.00)	(53.00)	(19.67)	(100.00)

Source: Field Data

Table - 5.3
AGE DISTRIBUTION OF SAMPLE RESPONDENTS

Name of the Village with Mandal	20-30	31-40	41-50	51-60	61 and above	Total
I. SHAYAMPET MANDAL						
1. Shayampet	8	20	12	-	-	40
2. Pathipaka	9	9	10	2	-	30
3. Taherpur	6	10	10	2	2	30
II. VENKATAPUR						
4. Laxmidevipet	12	18	8	2	-	40
5. Peddapur	8	9	10	2	1	30
6. Ramanujapur	7	10	10	3	-	30
III. NARMETTA						
7. Narmetta	9	19	10	2	-	40
8. Veldandi	10	10	8	1	1	30
9. Ammapur	9	10	9	2	-	30
Total	78	115	87	16	4	300
	(26.0)	(38.34)	(29.00)	(5.33)	(1.33)	(100.00)

Total (26.0)   (38.34)   (29.0)   (5.33)   (1.33)   (100.00)

Source: Field Data

Table- 5.4
THE AVERAGE FAMILY-SIZE AND OTHER POPULATION DETAILS

Name of the Village	No. of house-holds	No of persons in the households			Average size of family
		Male	Female	Total	
I. SHAYAMPET MANDAL					
1 Shayampet	40	106	109	215	5.37
2. Pathipaka	30	75	73	148	4.90
3. Taherpur	30	76	74	150	5.00
II. VENKATAPUR					
4. Laxmidevipet	40	111	109	220	5.50
5. Peddapur	30	81	76	157	5.23
6. Ramanujapur	30	78	75	153	5.10
III. NARMETTA					
7. Narmetta	40	101	100	201	5.02
8. Veldandi	30	76	72	148	4.90
9. Ammapur	30	73	69	142	4.73
Total	300 (100.00)	777 (50.65)	757 (49.35)	1534 (100.00)	

Source: Field Data

In Shayampet Mandal, the village Shayampet occupies first place as far as number of persons and family size of the house-holds are concerned which are 215 and 5.33 rerpectively. Laxmidevipet in Venkatapur Mandal and Narmetta village in Narmetta Mandal also occupy the first position with 220 and 201 persons and 5.50 and 5.02 average family size respectively. The total population in the sample households was worked out as 1536 of which 50.65 percent (778) are male population and 49.35 percent (758) are female. Of all the sample villages put together, female population (109) is slightly more than male population (106) only in Shayampet village. The Venkatapur Mandal occupies first position in respect to the total population of the sample house- holds. This works out to 530 persons, followed by 513 in Shayampet Mandal and 493 in Narmetta. The average size of the family of total house-holds (300) is worked out as 5.11.

WORKING PATTERN OF THE FAMILY MEMBERS OF SAMPLE HOUSE-HOLDS

Of the total 1536 family members, 698 (45.44%) are working and 838 (54.56%) are non-working population. The highest number of working population comes from Venkatapur Mandal which is 244 followed by 240 and 214 from Shayampet and Narmetta Mandals respectively. The highest non-working population is in Venkatapur Mandal i.e.286 persons followed by 279 and 273 from Narmetta and Shayampet Mandals.

Out of the total working population of 698 persons, the agricultural labourers category constitute a majority i.e. 213 persons; out of 300 followed by marginal farmers and rural artisans category with 183 and 175 persons and the lowest in 'others' occupation category. The highest work participation in agricultural labour category can be seen in Venkatapur Mandal.

Out of 213 working population among agricultural category, 77 are from this Mandal followed by Shayampet with 73 and Narmetta with 63. The number of non-working persons are high in the rural artisans category. Out of 838 non-working persons among the sample house-holds, 240 are in this category. Followed by marginal farmers with 222 persons and agricultural labour 192. The lowest non-working population among rural artisans the highest, 83, can be visualised from Shayampet Mandal followed by Venkatapur with 80 and Narmetta with 77 persons.

It is also evident from the above description that the working population is higher than the non-working population in case of agricultural labour families.

EDUCATIONAL PATTERN OF SAMPLE RESPONDENTS

Out of 300 respondents, 76 percent (228) are illiterates. The highest illiteracy is among agricultural labourers category followed by marginal farmers, rural artisans and others category. Of the total 72 literates, 53 are having primary education status and 19 are having secondary education. No respondent is having higher education. The highest literacy is among rural artisans. Others category, marginal farmers and agricultural labourers follow next.

EDUCATIONAL PATTERN OF THE FAMILY MEMBERS

Of the 1536 family members of the respondent house-holds, 478 (31.12%) are literates and 1058 (68.88%) are illiterates. The highest literacy is in Shayampet Mandal i.e 178 followed by Venkatapur and Narmetta Mandals with 162 and 138 respectively. The highest literacy is observed in case of rural artisans category followed by marginal farmers, agricultural labourers and others category. Out of the total literates, 166 are in rural artisans category, followed by 135 in marginal farmers, 89 in agricultural labourers and 88 in others category.

The percentage of sample house-hold population educated at primary level is as high as 72.38% (346 out of 478) followed by 23.22% and 4.39% at secondary and higher education levels respectively.

Out of 1058 total illiterates, Venkatapur Mandal accounts for 367 (34.69%) illiterates followed by Narmetta and Shayampet Mandals with 355 (33.56%) and 336 (31.75%) respectively. The highest illiteracy is among agricultural labourer category with 330 (31.61%) followed by 285 (27.02%), 282 (26.34%) and 161 (15.03%) among marginal farmers, rural artisans and others category respectively.

LAND HOLDING PARTICULARS OF SAMPLE HOUSE HOLDS

The unique feature of the land holding particulars is that 48 percent of respondents are landless i.e. 144 respondents out of 300 are having no land asset. 14 percent (42 respondents) are having land below 0.5 acres, 12.67 percent (38 respondents) belonged to the fractile group of 0.6-1.0 acre, 12.33 percent of respondents (37) are having land in the range of 1.1-2.0 acres and (39 respondents) 13.0 percent are in the fractile group of 2.1-3.0 acres are from marginal farmers category only. And between 1.1-2.0 acres also marginal farmers are as high as 33 (89.19%) out of the total respondents of 37 in this fractile group.

Table -5.5
LAND HOLDING PATTERN AMONG RESPONDENTS

S.No.	Particulars in Acres	M.F.	R.A.	A.L.	O.T.	Total
1.	Nil	-	54	48	41	143 (47.67)
2.	Below 0.5	-	12	18	11	41 (13.61)
3.	0.5-1	5	6	12	8	31 (10.33)
4.	1.1-2	21	6	-	6	33 (11.06)
5.	2.1-3	52	-	-	-	52 (17.33)
6.	3.1-4	-	-	-	-	- (6.33)
Total		78 (26.0)	78 (26.0)	78 (26.0)	66 (22.0)	300 (100.0)

The landless respondents are high in number among agricultural labourers category. Out of 144 landless respondents, 54

(37.50%) are from this category followed by rural artisans and others category with 49 (34.02%) and 41 (28.48%) respectively.

Out of 78 respondents selected from marginal farmers category, 72 percent are having land between 1-3 acres. Among rural artisans (78), agricultural labourers (78), and others category (66), 62.82%, 69.23% and 62.12% are having no land respectively.

In all the Mandals put together landless respondents are the highest in number. The highest landless respondents are in Shayampet Mandal with 51 (35.42%) among all categories except marginal farmers, followed by 49 (34.03%) and 44 (30.55%) in Venkatapur and Narmetta Mandals respectively.

In Sayampet and Venkatapur Mandals, agricultural labourers are more in number in landless group and rural artisans in Narmetta Mandal.

Among the land owning class the highest number are in Narmetta Mandal with 56 (35.90%) respondents followed by 51 (32.69%) and 49 (31.41%) in Venkatapur and Shayampet Mandals respectively. The marginal farmers having land between 1-3 acres are more in Venkatapur Mandal with 26 respondents out of 72 in this fractile group., followed by 23 marginal farmers both in Shayampet and Narmetta Mandals.

INCOME LEVELS OF SAMPLE RESPONDENTS

House holds among marginal farmers category are in first position in respect of average annual income, monthly income and per capita income. The marginal farmers are having the highest average monthly income of Rs. 541.70 followed by rural artisans, agricultural labourers and others category with an income of Rs. 550.02, 469.99 and 411.66 respectively.

The average per capita income of marginal farmers (Rs. 104.22) is the highest among all categories followed by rural artisans, agricultural laboureres with Rs. 99.67, 92.16, 91.36 respectively.

Table 5.6 shows income pattern of house holds by mandal-wise and category-wise. The highest average per capita income of all categories occurs in Vengkatapur Mandal (Rs. 99.59): the Sayampet Mandal is slightly behind with Rs. 98.45 per capita income and followed by Narmetta with Rs. 92.58. In average monthly income also the same position existing. Among various categories margin al farmers of Venkatapur are having highest per capita income of Rs. 107.42. The lowest position is in a agricultural labourers category of Narmetta Mandal with 88.12.

Table -5.6
INCOME PATTERN OF HOUSE-HOLDS

S.No.	Category	Shayampet Mandal			Venkatapur Mandal			Narmetta Mandal		
		Monthly income	Per capita income	Family size	Monthly income	Per capita income	Family size	Monthly income	Per capita income	Family size
1.	M.F.	558.40	105.36	5.30	583.29	107.42	5.44	483.41	99.88	4.84
2.	R.A.	560.69	103.45	5.42	546.00	104.00	5.26	483.38	91.55	5.28
3.	A.L.	463.12	93.75	4.94	516.51	94.60	5.47	457.34	88.12	5.19
4.	O.T.	443.47	91.25	4.86	454.41	92.36	4.93	397.11	90.46	4.39

Source: Field Data

The highest average monthly income is observed to have occurred among marginal farmers of Venkatapur Mandal with Rs. 583.29. The lowest monthly income is among others category Narmetta Mandal with Rs. 397.11. Venkatapur Mandal, comparatively has better irrigation facilities than the other Mandals and also has the highest income. The drought prone Narmetta Mandal is at the lowest position on the scale. In all categories the lowest income occurs in this Mandal only. The Shayampet's position lies in between these two.

EXPENDITURE PARTICULARS OF SAMPLE HOUSE-HOLDS

The following tables 5.7.1 and 5.7.2 show the per capita expenditure levels among sample house-holds by Mandal and category-wise.

Patterns of Rural Poverty: A Case Study of
Warangal District

Table - 5.10

AVERAGE MONTHLY CONSUMPTION EXPENDITURE AMONG SAMPLE HOUSE-HOLDS
SHAYAMPET MANDAL

S.No.	Category	Cereals	Vegeta-bles	Pulses	Poultry & Meat	Dairy Products	Oil	Miscella-neous	Total	Per capita consum-ption
1.	M.F.	248.75	35.75	20.61	21.33	17.68	16.17	11.46	372.14	75.86
		(66.84)	(9.61)	(5.53)	(5.73)	(4.76)	(4.46)	(3.07)	(100.0)	
2.	R.A.	257.85	44.69	21.03	23.38	13.78	18.30	15.41	394.40	82.21
		(65.37)	(11.33)	(5.33)	(5.94)	(3.49)	(4.64)	(3.90)	(100.0)	
3.	A.L.	218.28	29.92	16.00	18.65	7.71	14.12	10.37	315.05	59.85
		(69.28)	(9.50)	(5.08)	(5.92)	(2.48)	(4.48)	(3.29)	(100.0)	
4.	O.T.	215.92	29.17	16.45	18.30	8.77	12.74	10.93	312.28	68.98
		(69.14)	(9.34)	(5.27)	(5.86)	(2.81)	(4.08)	(3.50)	(100.0)	

Source: Field Data

Table -5.7.2
POVERTY LEVELS AMONG THE HOUSE-HOLDS

S.No.	Category	No. of households below the poverty line	Percentage	No. of households above the poverty line	Percentage
1.	M.F.	61	78.20	17	21.89
2.	R.A.	69	88.46	9	11.54
3.	A.L.	76	97.44	2	
4.	O.T.	66	100.00	-	-
	Total	272	90.69	28	9.31

Source: Field Data

It is evident from the table that, the highest concentration of the respondents is among the expenditure levels of Rs. 77-87, 87- 97 and 97-107. Of the total respondents, 76.67 percent are in this consumption range. Of these, the respondents from Shayampet Mandal are highest in number (34) followed by Venkatpur and Narmetta with 32 and 29 respectively. There are 230 respondents in the expenditure group of Rs. 87-97. In the consumption level of Rs. 77-107, highest percentage of 35.22(81) are from Narmetta Mandal followed by 32.61%(75) and 32.17% (74) from Venkatapur and Shayampet Mandals respectively.

Of the total respondents below the poverty line, 100 percent of the 'others' category are below the poverty line. 97.44 % of agricultural labourers, 88.46% rural artisans and 78.20% marginal farmers are under the poverty line. The respondents near to the poverty line(Rs.107.00) range of 97-107 highest (43.55%) are from Venkatapur Mandal with 27 respondents followed by (29.03%) 18 and (27.42%) 17 from Shayampet and Narmetta. Among these, marginal farmers are more in number with 22 respondents followed by 20,14 and 6 from rural artisans, agricultural labour and others category respectively. Of the total respondents who crossed the poverty line, highest are from marginal farmers category with 17 respondents (60.71%), followed by rural artisans and agricultural labourers with 9 (32.15%) and 2 (7.14%) respectively.

POVERTY LEVELS AMONG SAMPLE HOUSE-HOLDS

The following Table 5.8 illustrates the poverty levels among the population of the sample house-holds, on the basis of the table it can be noticed that the most of the house-hold population are in the monthly expenditure level between Rs. 77 and 107. Out of the total population of 1536 persons, 1176 are in this range. The total persons below the poverty line are 1393 constituting 90.69 percent of the total population among the sample house-holds. Of these 97.16 percent (479) are from Narmetta Mandal 88.10 percent (452) are from Shayampet and 87.16 percent (462) from Venkatapur. Of the total 143 persons above the poverty line, 68 are from Venkatapur Mandal, 61 are from Shayampet Mandal and 14 are from Narmetta Mandal.

Table -5.8
POVERTY LEVELS AMONG THE POPULATION OF THE SAMPLE
HOUSE-HOLDS

S.No.	Per capita exp. (in Rs.)	SHAYAM-PET MANDAL		VENKATA-PUR MANDAL		NARMETTA MANDAL		Total No. of house-holds	Total No. of per-sons	Perce-ntage
1	2	3	4	5	6	7	8	9	10	11
1.	47-57	1	5.13	2	10.61	1	4.93	4	20.66	1.34
2.	57-67	4	20.52	3	15.90	5	24.65	12	61.07	3.98
3.	67-77	9	46.17	7	37.10	10	49.30	26	132.57	8.63
4.	77-87	22	112.86	16	84.80	35	172.55	73	370.21	24.17
5.	87-97	34	174.42	32	169.60	29	142.97	95	487.00	32.78

1	2	3	4	5	6	7	8	9	10	11
6. 97-107	18	92.34	27	143.10	17	84.81	62	319.24	20.79	
7. 107-117	8	41.04	9	47.70	3	14.79	20	103.53	6.67	
8. 117-127	4	20.52	4	21.20	-	-	8	41.72	2.64	
Total	100	513.00	100	530.00	100	494.00	300	1536.00	100.00	

Source: Field Data

CONSUMPTION EXPENDITURE PATTERN

The consumption expenditure, in this study, is inclusive of expenditure on food and non-food items. The monthly consumption expenditure in this study is worked out on the basis of per capita consumption expenditure below the poverty line norm, formulated by the Seventh Five Year Plan. It is evident from Table 5.9 that among the three selected Mandals, Venkatapur registered the highest level of consumption expenditure followed by Shayampet and Narmetta. The marginal farmers category of the households from Venkatapur Mandal registered the highest monthly consumption expenditure of Rs. 579.27 among all the categories and Mandals, the lowest is in case of others category from Narmetta Mandal of Rs. 410.64. As mentioned earlier, the average per capita consumption expenditure of the all categories put together has been below the poverty line of Rs. 107 for rural areas as defined by the Planning Commission.

The highest per capita consumption expenditure is recorded among the marginal farmer category from Venkatapur Mandal and the lowest among agricultural labourers from Narmetta Mandal. Except rural artisans, all other categories have higher consumption expenditure from Venkatapur among all the Mandals. The rural artisans from Shayampet Mandal registered higher consumption expenditure than the other rural artisans from Venkatapur and Narmetta Mandals.

In all the three Mandals, the lowest consumption expenditure is recorded in case of others category. The percentage of consumption expenditure on food items is high among rural artisans category from

Narmetta Mandal, and the lowest from agricultural labourers category from Shayampet.

Average Monthly Consumption Expenditure Among Sample House-Holds

Shayampet Mandal

The following table 5.10 gives an account of pattern of average monthly consumption expenditure of sample households on food items.

In shayampet mandal rural artisans in comparison to all other categories have registered highest monthly consumption expenditure of Rs.394.40 on food items. The lowest is in case of others category. The major portion of the consumption on food items has been made on cereals. The percentage is 69.28. The next priority has been given to vegetables, followed by expenditure on poultry and meat products. Expenditure on this item is by and large similar with slight variation. It is also evident from the above table that where the per capita consumption is low the expenditure on cereals is also high. The agricultural labourers in this Mandal with low per capita consumption of Rs. 59.85 are spending a higher percentage on consumption of cereals. The spending a higher percentage on consumption of cereals. The 'vice-versa' can also be proved, as rural artisans with Rs.82.21 per capita consumption spending, low percentage of expenditure on cereals than other categories.

Table -5.9

AVERAGE MONTHLY CONSUMPTION PATTERN AMONG SAMPLE HOUSE-HOLDS

S.No.	Categ-ory	SHAYAMPET MANDAL				VENKATAPUR MANDAL				NARMETTA MANDAL			
		Food	Non-food	Total	Per capita consumption	Food	Non-food	Total	Per capita consumption	Food	Non-food	Total	Per capita consumption
1.	M.F.	372.44 (67.34)	180.49 (32.66)	552.63 (100.0)	104.27	393.90 (68.0)	185.37 (32.0)	579.27 (100.0)	106.68	330.12 (66.74)	164.53 (33.26)	494.65 (100.0)	102.20
2.	R.A.	394.40 (70.80)	162.67 (29.2)	557.07 (100.0)	102.78	365.81 (67.35)	177.35 (32.65)	543.16 (100.0)	103.46	347.40 (71.13)	141.00 (28.87)	488.40 (100.0)	92.50
3.	A.L.	315.05 (69.25)	135.90 (30.75)	450.95 (100.0)	95.76	368.17 (69.54)	161.28 (30.46)	529.45 (100.0)	96.97	314.19 (67.08)	154.20 (32.92)	468.39 (100.0)	90.25
4.	O.T.	312.28 (66.60)	138.67 (33.40)	450.95 (100.0)	92.79	313.43 (67.28)	152.44 (32.72)	465.87 (100.0)	94.67	282.35 (68.76)	128.29 (31.24)	410.64 (100.0)	93.45

Source : Field Data

Patterns of Rural Poverty: A Case Study of Warangal District

Table - 5.7.1

PER CAPITA EXPENDITURE PARTICULARS OF SAMPLE HOUSE-HOLDS

S.No.	Percapita expenditure (in Rs.)	SHAYAMPET MANDAL					VENKATAPUR MANDAL					NARMETTA MANDAL					TOTAL
		M.F.	R.A.	A.L.	O.T.	Total	M.F.	R.A.	A.L.	O.T.	Total	M.F.	R.A.	A.L.	O.T.	Total	
1.	47-57	-	-	-	1	1	-	-	-	2	2	-	-	-	1	1	4
2.	57-67	-	-	-	4	4	-	-	1	2	3	-	1	1	3	5	12
3.	67-77	-	2	2	5	9	-	1	2	4	7	1	1	3	5	10	26
4.	77-87	2	4	9	7	22	1	2	5	8	16	7	12	10	6	35	73
5.	87-97	11	9	10	4	34	8	9	11	4	32	9	8	8	4	29	95
6.	97-107	7	6	4	1	18	8	11	6	2	27	7	3	4	3	17	62
7.	107-117	4	3	1	-	8	6	2	1	-	9	2	1	-	-	3	20
8.	117-127	2	2	-	-	4	3	1	-	-	4	-	-	-	-	-	8
	Total	26	26	26	22	100	26	26	26	22	100	26	26	26	22	100	300

Source : Field Data

VENKATAPUR MANDAL

Table 5.11(See page 93) presents data relating to the average monthly consumption expenditure pattern of sample house-holds on food items.

In Venkatapur Mandal, marginal farmers are having highest consumption expenditure of Rs.393.90 and lowest is among 'other' category at Rs.313.43. The per capita consumption level is also high among marginal farmers and low among 'others'. Here also the expenditure on cereals is substantially high in percentage terms.

In case of 'others' category the per capita consumption expenditure (70.15) on cereals is high. Marginal farmers are spending 67.01 percentage of their total expenditure on cereals. Here also the second position is occupied by vegetables item. All the categories are spending more or less equally with slight variation on poultry and meat.

The agricultural labourers and rural artisans are spending 69.82 and 69.29 percentage of consumption expenditure on cereals. The expenditure on dairy product and oil is slightly high in the Venkatapur Mandal among all the categories.

NARMETTA MANDAL

The highest per capita consumption, as shown in table 5.12 (see page 94) is among rural artisans and the lowest is in case of others category. In this Mandal also, major percentage of expenditure was incurred on cereals. The highest percentage of expenditure on this item was registered in 'others' category. And the lowest in case of marginal farmers category. Respondents from this Mandal are also spending the second highest percentage of expenditure on vegetables followed by poultry and meat and pulses. The expenditure on dairy and oil is lower than that in other Mandals.

Though, there is no significant variation in consumption patterns among three Mandals, the percentage of expenditure on cereals is higher in Narmetta Mandal than in other two Mandals. And percentage of expenditure on nutritious items like pulses, poultry and dairy is low. The expenditure on these, is lower in Narmetta and Shayampet than in Venkatapur. Expenditure on oil is also less in

Narmetta Mandal, in all categories, than in the other two Mandals. The miscellaneous expenditure in all the three Mandals and among all the categories is the lowest in percentage terms.

The above figures relating to the consumption pattern of respondents by category-wise and mandal-wise in general, and on food items in particular, clearly indicate that, respondents with low income are spending much amount on food items in general and within food items on cereals in particular. Respondents, belonging to agricultural labourers and rural artisans categories, with their low per capita consumption levels are spending highest percentage amounts on cereals. Respondents of these categories are spending 69.28 %, 69.14 percent, 69.82, 70.15 and 71.38, 72.14 percent on cereals from Shayampet, Vekatapur and Narmetta Mandals respectively. The expenditure on nutrition items like, pulses, poultry and meat products and dairy products is low among these sections, when, compared to others.

Table- 5.11

AVERAGE MONTHLY CONSUMPTION EXPENDITURE ON FOOD ITEMS

VENKATAPUR MANDAL

(Value in Rs.)

S.No.	Category	Cereals	Vegeta-bles	Pulses	Poultry & Meat	Dairy Products	Oil	Miscella-neous	Total	Per capita Consump-tion
1.	M.F.	263.97 (67.01)	35.35 (8.97)	22.05 (5.60)	22.53 (5.72)	17.61 (4.47)	20.73 (5.26)	11.66 (2.96)	393.90 (100.0)	82.26
2.	R.A.	253.48 (69.29)	29.42 (8.04)	19.78 (5.41)	21.70 (5.93)	12.20 (3.35)	16.50 (4.51)	12.73 (3.47)	365.81 (100.0)	73.86
3.	A.L.	257.06 (69.82)	27.54 (7.48)	21.98 (5.97)	21.90 (5.95)	10.32 (2.80)	17.52 (4.76)	11.85 (3.22)	368.17 (100.0)	77.32
4.	O.T.	219.87 (70.15)	22.81 (7.28)	17.80 (5.68)	18.12 (5.78)	8.72 (2.78)	16.08 (5.13)	10.04 (3.20)	313.43 (100.0)	70.39

Source : Field Data

Patterns of Rural Poverty: A Case Study of Warangal District

Table- 5.12

AVERAGE MONTHLY CONSUMPTION EXPENDITURE ON FOOD ITEMS

NARMETTA MANDAL

(Value in Rs.)

S.No.	Category	Cereals	Vegeta-bles	Pulses	Poultry & Meat	Dairy Products	Oil	Miscella-neous	Total	Per capita Consump-tion
1.	M.F.	226.70 (68.67)	28.25 (8.56)	17.73 (5.37)	18.46 (5.59)	14.06 (4.26)	14.92 (4.52)	10.00 (3.03)	330.12 (100.0)	61.45
2.	R.A.	240.97 (69.31)	27.89 (8.03)	18.44 (5.31)	19.53 (5.62)	10.90 (3.14)	17.87 (5.14)	11.98 (3.45)	347.40 (100.0)	70.55
3.	A.L.	224.27 (71.38)	23.28 (7.41)	15.61 (4.97)	17.43 (5.55)	7.27 (2.31)	15.68 (4.99)	10.65 (3.39)	314.19 (100.0)	62.71
4.	O.T.	203.68 (72.14)	19.99 (7.08)	13.30 (4.71)	14.96 (5.30)	8.23 (2.91)	13.24 (4.69)	8.95 (3.17)	282.35 (100.0)	56.34

Source : Field Data

AVERAGE MONTHLY CONSUMPTION EXPENDITURE ON NON-FOOD ITEMS

SHAYAMPET MANDAL

The importance of non-food items in consumer expenditure basket is increasing in recent years among the poorer sections also. As the expenditure on non-food items among all the categories is between 29-32 percent of total consumption expenditure, expenditure on clothing is high among marginal farmers, rural artisans in Shayampet Mandal and others category. The agricultural labourers category is spending 25.15 percent of expenditure on liquors and tobacco. Liquors and tobacco among rural artisans and clothing among agricultural labourers is accorded the second preference. Expenditure on festivals and rituals is significant among all the categories, traveling expenditure is high among rural artisans and low among agricultural labourers. Expenditure on soaps and cosmetics is also in sizable percentage. This is also high among rural artisans (11.28%) followed by marginal farmers (8.62%) others (7.45%) and agricultural labour (6.19).

Expenditure on fuel and light is high among marginal farmers and rural artisans and very low among 'others' and agricultural labourers.

VENKATAPUR MANDAL

In this Mandal except rural artisans, respondents of all other categories are giving top priority to liquors and tobacco in their consumption pattern. The rural artisans are giving first preference to clothing while expenditure on liquors and tobacco got the second position among them. Of all the categories, respondents from agricultural labourers are spending highest percentage on liquors and tobacco. The lowest percentage is by marginal farmers. Expenditure on health and education has occupied third place in the consumption levels of marginal farmers and rural artisans. Agricultural labourers are spending third highest expenditure on festivals and rituals followed by health and education items. Spending on traveling is high among the rural artisans (8.13%) and others (8.14%) followed marginal farmers (6.94%) and agricultural labour (4.60%). Expenditure on soaps and cosmetics is also high among rural artisans (8.82%). Lowest expenditure lies among agricultural labourers. Consumption expenditure on fuel and light is high among marginal farmers category and lower among agricultural labourers.

NARMETTA MANDAL

Expenditure on liquors and tobacco got the highest priority in the consumption pattern among marginal farmers, agricultural labourers and 'others' category. Of these, agricultural labourers are spending highest percentage of expenditure of their total expenditure. Health and education items are given the first priority by rural artisans. Festivals and rituals are forming second position among the expenditure class of marginal farmers, agricultural labourers and others. The percentage of expenditure on traveling and soaps and cosmetics is high among rural artisans. The lowest is among agricultural labour regarding former, and among 'others' in latter item. Rural artisans and agricultural labourers are having a higher expenditure on both fuel and light and miscellaneous items.

The expenditure pattern in the three Mandals varies a little. While most of the respondents from Shayampet Mandal are having higher expenditure on clothing, the expenditure on liquors and tobacco is high in both Venkatapur and Narmetta Mandals. While the expenditure on miscellaneous items is the lowest in Venkatapur among all the categories except marginal farmers, the expenditure on fuel and light is lowest in Shayampet Mandal. Rural artisans from Shayampet Mandal are incurring highest expenditure on soaps and cosmetics (11.28%). The expenditure pattern on these items in other two Mandals is in between the range of 9.33% to 7.25% with slight variations. Irrespective of their total consumption expenditure or per capita consumption expenditure respondents of all categories from all the Mandals are spending highest amount on liquors and tobacco with an average expenditure of 21.24 percent, followed by, expenditure on clothing, health, education and festival and rituals with an average percentage of 19.79, 17.41 and 16.30 respectively.

The analysis, based on the study results, presented in the foregoing pages, points to the fact that, even as the government spending crores of rupees on anti-poverty programmes, the change in the living standards of poor and down trodden poverty stricken masses is very little. The factors responsible for this pathetic state of affairs could be traced to the structural maladies. In the villages of India, sizable percentage of earnings of rural masses are going again into the hands of richer sections (liquor contractors, traders, commission agents and money lenders etc.) The governmental programmes are not contributing much to the structural transformation.

ASSETS POSITION OF RESPONDENTS

More than half of the total 300 respondents (55.34%) have only huts to live in. The percentage of respondents living in huts is the highest in Narmetta Mandal (62%) followed by Venkatapur (59%) and Shayampet Mandals. Of the 166 sample respondents, who are living in huts, agricultural labourers out number other categories. Next come rural artisans and marginal farmers. Even the number of respondents, who do not possess their own house, is as much as 31 out of 300. Of them, 18 come from agricultural labour category. Of the total 300 sample respondents nearly 30 percent own a tiled house. Of there a majority come from Shayampet Mandal. Of the total sample respondents living in tile houses, marginal farmers are the highest in number i.e. 46 out of 89. Only 4.67 percent of the total respondents are living in pucca houses, out of which again marginal farmers are in majority. Only one respondent belonging to agricultural labourer category possessed a pucca house. In the relatively backward mandal, Narmetta, no respondent possesses either a tiled house or a pucca house.

PATTERN OF PRODUCTIVE ASSETS

As the figures in Table 5.13 indicate, the productive assets value of 86 out of 300 respondents is below Rs.500 worth. Of them 84 respondents are rural artisans. Of the total 300 respondents, 84 respondents do not possess any productive assets out of which agricultural labourers are 45. There are 44 respondents in the range of Rs.500-1000 assets value; of them 23 are rural artisans. Of the total 78 rural artisans 55 possess assets whose value is below Rs.1000.

Table -5.13
PATTERN OF PRODUCTIVE ASSETS
NARMETTA MANDAL

S.No.	Category	Nil	Below Rs. 500	501 to 1000	1001 to 1500	1501 to 2000	Above 2001	Total
1.	M.F.	-	10	8	24	9	27	78
2.	R.A.	9	32	23	6	5	3	78
3.	A.L.	45	23	8	2	-	-	78
4.	O.T.	30	21	5	6	4	-	66
Total		84	86	44	38	18	30	300
		(28.00)	(28.67)	(14.67)	(12.66)	(6.00)	(10.00)	(100.00)

Source:Field Data

The position of marginal farmers is relatively better as far as possession of productive assets is concerned. Out of the total 78 marginal farmers, 60 are in the range of Rs.1000-2000, and above 55 respondents out of 66 belonging to other categories possesses productive assets worth below Rs.500. In case of agricultural labourers category, 68 out of 78 i.e. 87.18% possess productive assets whose worth is below Rs.500.

MANDAL-WISE PATTERN OF PRODUCTIVITY ASSETS

The mandal-wise particulars of productivity assets are presented in Table -5.14. As it is evident from the information given in this table, the relative position of the respondents of Venkatapur Mandal is better than that of those coming from other mandals. The percentage respondents possessing productive assets is greater in Venkatapur Mandal which is 76 percent followed by Shayampet (71.0%) and Narmetta (69.0%). In all the three mandals the agricultural labourers possessing of productive assets is very negligible. With slight variation the relative position of marginal farmers, in all the three mandals, slightly better than those belonging to other categories. In all the three mandals most of the rural artisan respondents are in the range of Rs. 500-1000 assets value.

Table -5.14
MADAL-WISE PATTERN OF PRODUCTIVE ASSESTS
(Value in Rs.)

S.No	Category	SHAYAMPET MANDAL							VENKATAPUR MANDAL							NARMETTA MANDAL							Grand Total
		Nil	Below Rs. 500	501 to 1000	1001 to 1500	1501 to 2000	Above 2001	Total	Nil	Below Rs. 500	501 to 1000	1001 to 1500	1501 to 2000	Above 2001	Total	Nil	Below Rs. 500	501 to 1000	1001 to 1500	1501 to 2000	Above 2001	Total	
1.	M.F.	-	3	2	6	4	11	26	-	2	8	3	-	13	26	-	7	4	10	2	3	26	78
2.	R.A.	3	12	7	2	1	1	26	-	2	9	8	4	2	26	11	8	-	2	1	4	26	78
3.	A.L.	15	8	2	1	1	-	26	13	10	3	2	-	-	26	17	5	3	1	-	-	26	78
4.	O.T.	11	7	2	1	1	-	22	9	8	3	2	-	-	22	10	6	3	3	-	-	22	66
	Total	29	30	13	10	6	12	100	24	27	16	14	5	14	100	31	29	15	14	7	4	100	300

Source : Field Data

LIVE-STOCK ASSETS PARTICULARS

Table 5.15 presents the details of live-stock assets of the sample respondents. More than 50 percent (162 out of 300) of the total respondents do not possess any live-stock assets. Out of this, many are rural artisans. Out of the 96 respondents possessing live-stock assets in the range of Rs. 500-2000 worth 63 (65.62%) are marginal farmers. Most of the agricultural labourers and other respondents do not own any live-stock assets. Out of those whose live-stock asset value in below Rs. 500 many are agricultural labourers.

Table 5.15
LIVE-STOCK ASSETS PARTICULARS
(Values in Rs.)

S.No.	Category	Nil	Below Rs. 500	501 to 1000	1001 to 1500	1501 to 2000	Above 2001	Total
1.	M.F.	9	11	17	21	7	13	78 (26.0)
2.	R.A.	63	7	4	-	3	1	78 (26.0)
3.	A.L.	48	15	6	4	5	-	78 (26.0)
4.	O.T.	42	9	4	8	3	-	66 (22.0)
	Total	162 (54.0)	42 (14.0)	31 (10.33)	33 (11.0)	18 (6.0)	14 (4.67)	300 (100.00)

Source: Field Data

MANDAL WISE PATTERN OF LIVE-STOCK ASSETS

Many of the respondents from Narmetta Mandal are relatively in a disadvantageous position as far as live-stock assets are concerned as the data presented in Table 5.16 (see page 103) reveals. Out of the 162 total respondents who do not possess any live-stock assets 40.74

percent i.e. 66 respondents are from this mandal followed by 51 (31.48%) in Venkatapur and 45 (27.78%) in Shayampet Mandal. The percentage of respondents who have some live-stock assets in the highest in Shayampet Mandal (55) followed by Venkatapur (49) and Narmetta (34).

In all the three mandals, rural artisans are more in numbers who do not possess any live-stock assets. Out of the total 78 respondents of this category, nearly 80 percent do not own any live-stock assets.

Among the total marginal farmer respondents of 78, the percentage of respondents possessing live-stock assets is as high as 88.46 percent, followed by Venkatapur and Narmetta Mandals.

Most of the agricultural labourers and others from Narmetta Mandal are deprived of live-stock assets, compared to these categories in other mandals. In Narmetta, except marginal farmers, barring 1 from agricultural labourers category, no respondents is in possession of assets beyond Rs. 1000 worth.

HOUSE-HOLD ASSETS PARTICULARS

The data pertaining to the domestic assets of sample respondents are presented in Table 5.17 (see page 104), of the total 300 respondents, 223 i.e. 78.33 percent are having domestic assets in the value range of Rs. 500-1500 out of which 65 (27.66%) are marginal farmers, followed by 62 (26.38%) agricultural labourers, 60 (25.53%) rural artisans and 48 (20.43%) others.

As far as the number of respondents, who have some domestic assets, marginal farmers are the highest in number, followed by rural artisans, agricultural labourers and other category respondents. Most of the marginal farmers possess house-hold assets in the value range of Rs. 1000-1500. Only 15, out of the total 300 respondents possess domestic assets above the worth of Rs. 2000.

Table -5.16
MANDAL-WISE PATTERN OF LIVE-STOCK ASSETS

(Value in Rs.)

SHAYAMPET MANDAL

S.No.	Category	Nil	Below Rs. 500	501 to 1000	1001 to 1500	1501 to 2000	Above 2001	Total
1.	M.F.	-	2	7	9	2	6	26
2.	R.A.	19	2	2	0	2	1	26
3.	A.L.	14	5	3	0	4	0	26
4.	O.T.	12	1	1	6	2	0	22
	Total	45	10	13	15	10	7	100

VENKATAPUR MANDAL

S.No.	Category	Nil	Below Rs. 500	501 to 1000	1001 to 1500	1501 to 2000	Above 2001	Total
1.	M.F.	3	4	5	8	3	3	26
2.	R.A.	21	3	1	1	0	0	26
3.	A.L.	14	6	2	3	1	0	26
4.	O.T.	13	3	3	1	2	0	22
	Total	51	16	11	13	6	3	100

NARMETTA MANDAL

S.No.	Category	Nil	Below Rs. 500	501 to 1000	1001 to 1500	1501 to 2000	Above 2001	Total	Grand Total
1.	M.F.	6	5	5	4	2	4	26	78
2.	R.A.	23	2	1	0	0	0	26	78
3.	A.L.	20	4	1	1	0	0	26	78
4.	O.T.	17	5	0	0	0	0	22	66
	Total	66	16	7	5	2	4	100	300

Source : Field Data

Table -5.17
HOUSE-HOLD ASSETS PARTICULARS

(Values in Rs.)

S.No.	Category	Nil	Below Rs. 500	501 to 1000	1001 to 1500	1501 to 2000	Above 2001	Total
1.	M.F.	-	3	21	44	3	7	78 (26.0)
2.	R.A.	-	5	42	18	5	8	78 (26.0)
3.	A.L.	-	13	50	12	3	-	78 (26.0)
4.	O.T.	-	10	39	9	8	-	66 (22.0)
	Total	-	31 (10.33)	152 (50.67)	83 (27.67)	19 (6.33)	15 (5.00)	300 (100.00)

Source:Field Data

MANDAL-WISE HOUSE-HOLD ASSETS

Table 5.18 contains the mandal-wise data relating to the domestic assets. As far as the percentage of respondents having domestic assets, Shayampet Mandal stands first followed by Venkatapur and Narmetta Mandals. In all the three sample mandals, marginal farmer respondents are more in number in the possession of domestic assets. Rural artisans from Shayampet Mandal are relatively better placed.

Agricultural labourers and others category respondents do not possess domestic assets above the value of Rs. 2000 in any of the three mandals. The relative position of the respondents from Narmetta Mandal is worse than the other two mandals. Most of the respondents whose domestic asset value is below Rs. 500 are agricultural labourers and others category respondents.

Patterns of Rural Poverty: A Case of Warangal District

Table - 5.18

MANDAL-WISE PARTICULARS OF DOMESTIC ASSETS

(Value in Rs.)

S.No.	Category	SHAYAMPET MANDAL							VENKATAPUR MANDAL							NARMETTA MANDAL							Grand Total
		Nil	Bel-ow Rs. 500	501 to 1000	1001 to 1500	1501 to 2000	2001 & above	To-tal	Nil	Bel-ow Rs. 500	501 to 1000	1001 to 1500	1501 to 2000	2001 & above	To-tal	Nil	Bel-ow Rs. 500	501 to 1000	1001 to 1500	1501 to 2000	2001 & above	To-tal	
1.	M.F.	-	6	16	1	3	-	26	1	5	16	1	3	-	26	2	10	12	1	1	-	26	78
2.	R.A.	-	12	8	2	4	-	26	2	13	5	2	4	-	26	3	17	5	1	-	-	26	78
3.	A.L.	3	14	6	3	-	-	26	4	17	5	-	-	-	26	6	19	1	-	-	-	26	78
4.	O.T.	1	10	5	6	-	-	22	3	13	4	2	-	-	22	6	16	-	-	-	-	22	66
	Total	4	42	35	12	7	-	100	10	48	30	5	7	-	100	17	62	18	2	1	-	100	300

Source : Field Data

TEMPORARY MIGRATION PARTICULARS OF RESPONDENTS

In the analysis of rural poverty, it is essential to know whether the rural work force are getting sufficient employment locally or migrating to other places. Data were collected about the temporary migration particulars of the sample respondents and presented in table 5.19.

Table -5.19
TEMPORATY MIGRATION PARTICULARS OF RESPONDENTS

S.No.	Category	Not-migrated	Migrated	Total
1	M.F	68	10	78
2	R.A	44	34	78
3	A.L	38	40	78
4	O.T	52	10	66
	Total	202 (67.33)	94 (32.67)	300 (100.00)

Source: Field Data

As the data reveals, 98 out of 300 i.e. 32.67% respondents are migrating to other places in search of employment during the off seasons. Of these 98 respondents, 40 (40.81%) are agricultural labourers, 34 (34.69%) are rural artisans, 14 (14.28%) are other and 10 (10.22%) are marginal farmers. The degree of migration is high among agricultural labourers and low among marginal farmers.

MANDAL-WISE PARTICULARS OF TEMPORARY MIGRATION

Table 5.20 contains the mandal-wise details of the temporary migration of the sample respondents. It is evident from the figures presented in this table that migration is high in the backward areas. Out of the total 98 sample migrants of 44 (44.90%)are from the backward Narmetta Mandal. The corresponding figures in the other two mandals are 38 (38.77%) and 16 (16.33%) in Shayampet and Venkatapur Mandals respectively.

While migration is observed to be high among agricultural labourers. Among the three mandals, Narmetta Mandal registered highest migration among agricultural labourers. It is also observed that in this case, the percentage of agricultural labourers out of the total migrants is the highest in the backward mandal of Narmetta followed by Shayampet and Venkatapur Mandals with 15 and 4 agricultural labourer migrants respectively.

The summary of the findings and conclusions of the field study conducted are presented in the next chapter.

Table-5.20
MANDAL-WISE PARTICULARS OF TEMPORARY MIGRATION

		SHAYAMPET MANDAL			VENKATAPUR MANDAL			NARMETTA MANDAL		
S.No.	Category	Not-migrated	Mig-rated	Total	Not-migrated	Mig-rated	Total	Not-migrated	Mig-rated	Total
1.	M.F.	26	-	26	24	2	26	18	26	78
2.	R.A.	10	16	26	18	8	26	16	26	78
3.	A.L.	11	15	26	22	4	26	5	26	78
4.	O.T.	15	7	22	20	2	22	17	22	66
Total		62	38	100	84	16	100	56	100	300

Source: Field Data

6
SUMMARY AND CONCLUSIONS

The mass poverty that we are witnessing in India today, has its roots in the colonial rule, which went on for over a period of 200 years. The policies, implemented by the Britishers regarding land system, rural industries, education, services and other areas against the wishes of people on land increased immensely due to the destroyed rural industries and handicrafts, economic growth came to a near standstill in all fronts which increased the pauperisation of the country in general and rural areas in particular. Denudation of resources led the country to depend on foreign assistance to fulfill the basic requirements of the society. The freedom struggle which as only political dimensions in the earlier stages, taken into account the social-economic impacts of colonial rule in the later period. The ever increasing misery of rural life led the movement to be some what militant and more conscious, which ultimately resulted in the freedom for the Nation. At the time of independence the sufferings of the rural masses were on the peak level. Poverty, unemployment, shortage of food-grains and all other essential commodities were tottering the rural economy. The dichotomy of rural-urban also emerged during this period. Concentration of land holdings and deprivation of access to socio-economic assets not only increased the poverty but also inequalities.

With the advent of planning era, Government of India realised the plight of vast rural masses who did not have assets, guaranteed employment and the minimum living resources, and formulated various programmes to find out solution to the basic issues. These include land-reforms, green revolution, Nationalisation of Banks and a host of other anti-poverty programmes which are aimed at tackling the problem of poverty and rural development in a direct and more conceived manner.

Poverty as a concept is closely related to inequality and may also be identified with unemployment. There are two major problems involved in defining the concept of poverty. The first relates to the problem of identifying the poor and the second is the problem of measurement. Rowntree and Arshansky have tried to evolve a clear approach to define poverty on the basis of expenditure on necessities of life.

There are two broad concepts of poverty: relative poverty and absolute poverty. While relative poverty is measured in terms of inequality in the income distribution, absolute poverty is reckoned in terms of some kind of notion of subsistence considered appropriate to circumstances in the country concerned.

Any attempt, directed towards finding a solution to the problem of poverty should be backed with a proper methodology and application. Without a constructive frame-work regarding policy formulation, the success rate will be very low. Hence, it is necessary at the out-set to have thorough understanding on the problem of poverty. Proper mechanism has to be evolved to measure the extent of poverty. In this regard, various economists, social scientists, government organisation and independent researchers like Dandekar and Rath, Sukhatme, Ahluwalia, Bardhan, Krishnaji, C.T. Curien etc. had developed different methodologies and approaches to measure the poverty levels. Of these, caloric in-take norm is most significant. Though it has become a debatable issue among economists, it has its own merits and demerits. The growing concern among the various individuals and agencies is to evolve a workable methodology which throws a proper light into the thoughts and directions aimed at formulating policies to eradicate poverty. Inclusion of non-food items in the consumption expenditure basket, which is the measuring rod of poverty line is gaining momentum in recent years. Though Dandekar and Rath considered the expenditure on non-food items is more concerned to richer sections, factual evidence prove that, it is also concerned to the poor. Expenditure on clothing, housing, education, cosmetics, travelling and liquor and tobacco is forming into a formidable percentage of total consumption expenditure.

The policy programmes initiated in the early 70's and later have not succeeded to uplift the bottom deciles of the rural poor and to restructure the rural economy. This can be attributed to the nature of programmes, which lacked farsightedness and pragmatism. In the light of the past experience, Integrated Rural Development Programme came into the rural areas in full-fledged manner in the later part of 1980. Though this programme is formulated in a more constructive manner both in identifying the 'poor' and in providing the assistance to the beneficiaries, it failed to achieve the required targets. This is due to lack of co-ordination among various agencies that are involved in the implementation part.

During Seventh Five Year Plan, efforts have been made to integrate employment oriented programmes (NREP & RLEGP) into Jawahar Rojgar Yojana (JRY). In the Eighth Five Year Plan more emphasis is being layed on the implementation of anti-poverty programmes in accordance with overall economic development of the country. This plan also declared its shift towards employment oriented approach.

Micro-level studies on poverty are available from the studies conducted by Raviverma, Kumar, Gupta, Mishra, Radhakrisna and Mahajan. As the incidence of poverty as its root in endowment of resources and their proper utilisation, agro-climatic conditions and unemployment, which vary from region to region, there is every necessity to study regional pattern of poverty levels. Studies on levels of living in Andhra Pradesh, though limited in number have made a significant contribution to the micro-level analysis of the poverty. The works by B. Someshwar Rao, G. Parthasarathi, Perraju Sharma, Prof. Radha Krishna and K.Hanumanth Rao and K.V.S. Shastry, Radhakrishna and others estimated the incidence of poverty for the three regions viz Coastal Andhra, Rayalaseema and Telangana as 39 percent, 50 percent 49 percent respectively.

The extensive study undertaken by Prof. Radhakrishna and others reveal the poverty levels among the districts of Andhra Pradesh. They concluded that the variation in rural poverty across classes is more pronounced than across the regions. Warangal district, which selected for the present field study has been ranked three from the bottom both in per capita expenditure and G.D.P. In this district a staggering 72.80 percent of the rural population is below the poverty line.

Assuming the stability in the growth rate achieved during the Seventh Plan period, Eighth Plan approach paper hopefully or to say ambitiously envisages to bring down the percentage of people below the poverty line from the present level to 10 percent by 1990, and to completely eradicate poverty by the turn of the century i.e. 2000 A.D. But those who are in constant touch with the on- going evaluation studies on impact of various poverty-eradication and rural development programmes are not in any way ready to share, or to be a part of the thinking. Post independence economic development scenerio strengthens our apprehensions and this is also backed by the evaluative studies undertaken by independent researchers. A working paper prepared by Prof. Hanumanth Rao, S.P. Gupta and K.L. Dutta dwelt with the macro- economic implications of poverty eradication in India by 2000 A.D. If the so called 'zero level' poverty target set by Eighth Plan approach is to be realised, then there should be a major shift in the present level growth rate and productivity levels. This paper estimated that a zero level poverty situation in the economy needs 14 percent of growth rate of G.D.P. from the present 5 percent, the gross irrigated area to be 110.9 million hectares from the present 62.8 million hectares, fertilizer consumption is to be increased from 8.4 million tonnes to 21.11 million tonnes and the food-grains production to 246 million tonnes from 150 million tonnes of 1984-85.

The implications of the above study cast a shadow on the projections made by Eighth Plan approach to bring down the poverty level to a zero position in an economy with a poor record in the past, in the achievement of growth targets.

It is, thus, very essential to continously evaluate and estimate the possible trends and patterns of poverty in general and rural poverty in particular. The present study is undertaken with this as its main objective.

The present empirical study has been conduted in 9 villages of three Mandals of Warangal district with a sample size of 300 rural poor house-holds. Primary data were collected, through combined methods of personal interviews with the respondents with the help of a structured questionnaire. Information relating to the socio-economic background, levels of income, consumption and asset structures was collected and analysed. In the course of analysis the spatial aspects of the rural poverty were emphasised. The results of the field study are summarised below:

1. The working pattern among the family members of the sample house-holds reveals that, out of the total 1536 family members, 698 are working and 838 are non-working population, this works out 45.44 percent and 54.36 percent. The Venkatapur Mandal records the highest number of working population with 244 followed by Shayampet and Narmetta with 240 and 214 respectively. Among the categories, the highest work participation comes from agricultural labourers category with 213 working out of the total working population of 698. The non-working population is high among rural

artisans category with 240, out of 838 non-working population. Most of the school going children are found assisting their parents during the season in agricultural activities and during off-season in construction and allied works.

2. The literacy level of the respondents as well as the family members of the sample house-holds is very low. Out of 300 respondents, 76.0 percent are illiterates i.e. the literacy among the respondents is 24 percent only. Among the family members, 68.88 percent are illiterates and 31.2 percent are literates. The highest literacy can be seen from Shayampet Mandal and the highest illiteracy is in Venkatapur Mandal. Among the categories, the highest illiteracy can be attributed to the living conditions of this category. All the family members including children have to work throughout the year for their livelihood. This results in large-scale drop-outs.

3. The unique feature in the land holding pattern, in this study area is that, 48 percent of respondents are landless i.e. 144 respondents out of 300 are having no land asset. The landlessness is high among agricultural labourers category. Out of 144 landless respondents, 54 are from this category. The landless respondents are high in number in Shayampet Mandal, the other categories in this Mandal with meagre land asset, the landlessness is high. Though Narmetta Mandal constitute a highest number of land owning respondents, as earlier said, the recurring drought has virtually deprived the benefits that have to accrue.

4. The income levels of sample respondents worked out by this study reveal that the marginal farmers category is having highest average monthly income of Rs. 541.70 followed by rural artisans, agricultural labourers and others category with an income of Rs. 530.02, 469.99 and 411.66 respectively. The average per capita income is also high for marginal farmers (Rs. 104.22), among all categories. The agricultural labourers are lower on the income scale with a per capita income of Rs. 91.36.

The Venkatapur Mandal having a relatively better

irrigation facility has recorded the highest average monthly income, i.e. Rs.583.29 among marginal farmers. The lowest income level among all the categories can be seen from drought prone Narmetta Mandal.

5. The consumption expenditure levels of the respondents house -holds are such that most of the respondents (230 out of 300) are in the expenditure group Rs.87-97 which is much lower to the poverty line. All the respondents (100.0 percent) from 'others' category fall below the poverty line. And 97.44 percent of agriculture labourers, 88.46 percent of rural artisans and 78.20 percent of marginal farmers are below the poverty line.

   Among the family members of the sample house-holds, 1393 persons out of 1536 are below the poverty line. That works out of 90.69 percent. The poverty is more vulnerable in the Narmetta Mandal. 97.16 percent of persons from sample house-holds are below the poverty line.

   Out of total 300 respondents only 28 have crossed the poverty line. Of these 17 are from marginal farmers, 9 from rural artisans and 2 from agricultural labourers category.

   A further probe into the consumption expenditure pattern among the sample house-holds reveals that the Venkatapur among the three selected mandals, has registered highest level of consumption expenditure from all the categories. The marginal farmers category from Venkatapur Mandal has registered the highest monthly consumption expenditure of Rs.579.27 among all the categories and of all the mandals. The lowest is in the case of 'others' category from Narmetta Mandal of Rs.410.64.

6. The average consumption expenditure on food items is substantially as high as 68 percent of the total consumption expenditure incurred by all the categories from all the mandals. Rural artisans from Shayampet and Narmetta Mandals and agricultural labourers from Venkatapur Mandal incurring highest expenditure on food items among all the categories. Among the food

items, expenditure on cereals is in a formidable proportion in case of all the categories and all the mandals. Rural artisans from Shayampet and Narmetta Mandals and agricultural labourers from Venkatapur Mandal are incurring highest expenditure on cereals.

Most of the respondents from all the categories in the three mandals spend more on liquors and tobacco as the part of consumption expenditure on non-food items. The respondents from agricultural labourers category are spending highest amount on liquors and tobacco in all the mandals. The next priority is the clothing item to most of the respondents. The third preference has been given to expenditure on health and education by all the respondents from Shayampet and Venkatapur Mandals, while expenditure on, festivals and rituals is for the respondents of Narmetta. Major proportion of the expenditure on non-food items is going into unproductive channel.

7. The study on housing pattern shows that out of total 300 respondents, 55.34 percent are living in huts only. The highest (62%) percentage of respondents from Narmetta Mandal are living in huts. 31 respondents do not own a house. 30 percent of respondents are living in tiled houses and most of these are in Shayampet Mandal. Only 14 respondents are having pucca houses. Out of 166 respondents who are living in huts, 59 are from agricultural labourers category. The respondents who are living in huts and tiled houses are not having proper facilities like drinking water, sanitary and flooring.

8. Out of the total 300 respondents, 84 do not have productive assets. Most of the respondents from agricultural labourers category (45 out of 78) are not in possession of productive assets. 130 respondents out of 300 are owning productive assets (tools and implements) worth of Rs.1000 and below. This works to 43.24 percent. The respondents who are having productive assets worth of Rs.1501 and above are only 48. Out of these 36 are from marginal farmers category. 76 percent of the respondents from Venkatapur Mandal are having productive assets,

which is the highest one. In Narmetta Mandal 69 percent of the respondents are having productive assets which is the lowest one.

This study further reveals that, 235 respondents out of the total 300 (78.33%) have domestic assets in the value range of Rs.500- 1500. Most of the marginal farmers possess house-holds assets in the value range of Rs.1001-15-(44 out of 78). Respondents from marginal farmers and rural artisans category are only having house-hold assets worth of Rs.2001 and above. Out of 15 respondents in this range, 8 are from rural artisans and 7 from marginal farmers.

9.   The study area is deprived even of the basic facilities like health, education, potable water and roads. The migration tendency is high from Narmetta and Shayampet Mandals. The frequently recurring drought, forcible expenditure on festivals and ritual are forcing the respondents to go for unproductive loans at exorbitant interest rates from local money lenders. The debt burden and unemployment are the prime dual causes for migration from Shayampet Mandal. People from drought prone Narmetta Mandal are migrating temporarily to the far off places in search of their lively-hood.

The poverty among the rural poor is still in alarming proportions. Limited access to the productive assets, large scale unemployment, predominance of agriculture, poor health, education and transportation, low income and consumption levels among the poor, are the common features of our rural economy with slight variations in the intensity across the nation. Planning era which witnessed the implementation of various poverty eradication programmes hasn't made much dent in to the basic issues.

Food, shelter, protected drinking water, sanitation and the other basic requirements are still deprived to the vest sections of the rural masses.

A country's economic development, not merely depends on the increase in the G.N.P., but on the proper distribution in such a manner that majority of the rural masses get more access to the productive assets. The follow-up mechanism should be strengthened to see the implementation of various programmes that are initiated for eradicating poverty to be more prudent. The structural bottle-necks that are in the way of upliftment of the poor should be removed through active and prompt implementation of programmes in this direction.

Multi-pronged activities and approaches that are inclusive of all aspects covering the basic necessities of rural poor should be evolved and implemented vigorously with a clear direction.

An equitable distribution of land, formation of durable productive assets and community development programmes, governmental assistance to the poorer sections in various stages to realise their rights on newly created assets and to reap the benefits from them, are the basic programmes to be completed immanently to change rural set-up from present position. Along with the above activities, mass literacy, provision of proper health care, transportation, banking and other services will transform the present socio-economic set-up into a more dynamic one. In this context, one should not forget the importance of rural industrialisation, which relieves the pressure on land and provides long-term employment opportunities which in course of time will eradicate unemployment (including disguised unemployment). Thus, a more comprehensive policy frame-work of this type along with the implementation of these programmes in a more stringent and scientific manner only will help the down trodden to come out from the clutches of poverty, which, will enhance the prospects of economic development.

SELECT BIBLIOGRAPHY

1. Antsey, Verna   :   The Economic Development of India,
                               Longman's, London,1936.

2. Atkinson, A.B   :   The Economics of Inequality, Oxford
                               University Press, 1970.

3. Baden Powell, B.H   :   "The Indian Village Community", with
                               special reference to the Physical,
                               Enthrographic and Historical
                               Condition of India, Cosmo
                               Publications, New-Delhi, 1972

4. Bandyopadhyaya, J   :   Climate and World Order; An Inquiry
                               into the Natural Cause of
                               Underdevelopment, South Asian,
                               New-Delhi and Humanities Press,
                               Atlantic Islands, 1983.

5. Bandyopadhyaya, J   :   The Poverty of Nations- A Global
                               Perspective of Mass Poverty in the
                               Third World, Allied Publishers,
                               New-Delhi, 1988.

6. Baran Paul. A   :   The Political Economy of Growth
                               Monthly Review Press, New York,
                               1957.

7. Bhaduri, Amith   :   The Economic Structure of Backward
                               Agriculture, Academic Press Inc,
                               (London), 1983.

8. Chowdary, Prameth   :   The Indian Economy: Poverty and
                               Development, Vikas Publishing House
                               Pvt. Ltd., Bombay, 1978.

9. Dalip, S. Takur : Poverty, Inequality and Unemployment in Rural India, Some Conceptual and Methodological Issues in Measurement, B.R. Publishing Corporation, Delhi, 1985.

10. Dandekar, V.M. and
    Rath, Nilakantha : Poverty in India, Indian School of Political Economy, Poona, 1971.

11. Digby, William : Prosperous British India: A Revelatin from Official Records, T.Fisher Unwin, London, 1902.

12. Dutt, R.C : Economic History of India in the Victorian Age, Vol. 2, Seventh Edition, Routledge and Kegan Paul, London, 1950.

13. Dutt,Rudder and
    Sundaram, K.P.M : Indian Economy, S.Chand, New-Delhi, 1988.

14. Dutt, R.P : India Today and Tomorrow, People's Publishing House, New-Delhi, 1955.

15. Elliot, Charles : Patterns of Poverty in the Third World, Praeger Publishers, New York, 1975.

16. Galbraith, J.K : The Nature of Mass Poverty, Harward University Press, Cambridge, Mass, 1979.

17. Griffin, Keith : Land Concentration and Rural Poverty, Macmillan Press, 1976.

18. Hajela, T.N : History of Economic Thought, Shivalal
Agarwal Company, Agra, 1977.

19. Huq, Mahbubul : The Poverty Curtain: Choices for the
Third World, Colambia Unviversity
Press, New-York, 1978.

20. Jones,S;Joshi, P.C.
and Murmis, (Ed.) : "Rural Poverty and Agrarian Reforms",
Allied Publishers, New- Delhi, 1981.

21. Kurien, C.T : Poverty, Planning and Social
Transformation, Allied Publishers,
1978.

22. Laxminarayana,H. and
Tyagi, S.S : Changes in Agrarian Structure in India.
Agricole Publishing Acadamy,
New-Delhi, 1982.

23. Mahender Reddy, J,
and Yadava Reddy M.
etc. : Seventh Five Year Plan, Performance
and Perspective, Sterling Publication
Pvt. Ltd., New-Delhi, 1989.

24. Marx, Karl and
Engles, F : The Poverty of Philosophy, Progress
Publishers, Moscow, 1955.

25. Mellor, J.W. and
Desai, G.M : Agricultural Changes and Rural
Poverty, Oxford University Press,
Delhi, 1986.

26. Mishra, A.P : Rural Poverty in India: Problems in Planning and Strategy for Poverty Alleviation, Deep and Deep Publications, New-Delhi, 1988.

27. Murthy,N.L. and
Narayana, K.V : Rural Economy of India, Mittal Publications, New-Delhi. 1989.

28. Myrdal,Gunnar : Asian Drama: An Inquiry into the Poverty of Nations, Pantheon, New York, 1968. Vol.I and II.

29. Myrdal, Gunnar : The Challange of World Poverty, Penguin Publishers, 1970.

30. Naoroji, Dadabhai : Poverty in India, Winckworth Houlger and Company, the Aldine Press, London, 1988. Also see Poverty in India Then and Now: 1870-1970, by M.L. Dantwala, The Macmillan Co. of India Ltd., Delhi, 1973.

31. Naoroji, Dadabhai : Poverty and Un-British Rule in India, Swan Sonnenschein, London, 1901.

32. Nurkse, Ragnar : Problems of Capital Formation in Underdeveloped Countries, Basil Blackwell, Oxford, 1953.

33. Pant, A.D and
Tiwari, G.C (Ed.) : Planning and The Rural Poor, The Technical Publishing House, Allahabad, 1987.

34. Prasad, Kamata   :   Planning for Poverty Alleviation,
                                Agricultural Publishing Acadamy,
                                New-Delhi, 1985.

35. Radha Krishna, R.,
    Sastry,S.A.R,
    Sudhakar Reddy,S
    Mitra,G.K   :   Levels of Living in a State Setting,
                                Concept Publishing Company,
                                New-Delhi. 1989.

36. Jones, S.and
    Murmis, (Ed.)   :   "Rural Poverty and Agrarian Reform",
                                Allied Publishers, New- Delhi, 1981.

37. Rudra, Ashok   :   "Emerging Class Structure in Rural
                                India" in Srinivasan and Bardhan (ed),
                                1988.

38. Sanyal,S.K   :   "Trends in Landing and Poverty in
                                Rural India" in Srinivasan and Bardhan
                                op.cit.

39. Sen, Amartya   :   Poverty and Famines: An Essay on
                                Entilement and Derivation, Clarendon
                                Press, Oxford, 1981.

40. Singh, Charan   :   India's Poverty and its Soultion, Asia
                                Publishing House, Bombay, 1959.

41. Singh, Tarlok   :   Poverty and Social Change, with a
                                Reappraisal, Orient Longmans,
                                Bombay, 1969.

42. Srinivasan, T. N. and
    Bardhan, P.K. (Ed.) : Poverty and Income Distribution in
    India, Statistical Publishing Society,
    Calcutta, 1974.

43. Sushma Sagar : Poverty Measurement: Some Issues,
    RBSA Publishers, Jaipur, 1988.

44. Thorner, Alice and
    Daniel : Land and Labour in India, Asia
    Publishing House, Bombay, 1962.

45. Todaro, Michael : Economic Development in the Third
    World, Longman, New- York, 1981.

46. Town Send, Peter : The Concept of Poverty, Heinmann,
    London, 1970.

JOURNALS AND REPORTS

1. Ahluwalia. M.S   :   "Rural Poverty and Agricultural Performance in India", The Journal of Development Studies, April,1978.

2. Apsu, P.S   :   "Tenancy Reform in India", EPW, Special No. 1975.

3. Arshansky, M   :   "Counting the Poor: Another Look at the Poverty Profile", Social Security Bulletin, 28, quoted in A.B.Atkinson: The Economics of Inequlity,Oxford University Press,1975.

4. Atkinson, A.B   :   "On the Measurement of Inequality", Journal of Economic Theory, Vol.II, 1970.

5. Bagchi, A.K   :   "An Economic Policy for the New Government", EPW, Vol.xxv, No.6, Feb,1990.

6. Balakrishna, S   :   "Incidence of Rural Poverty in Recent Years". Behavioural Sciences and Economic Development, Vol.III, No.1, January, 1981, Hyderabad.

7. Bardhan, P.K   :   "On the Minimum Level of living and the Rural Poor", Indian Economic Review, 1970.

8. Bardhan, P.K   :   "On the Incidence of Poverty in Rural India", EPW, Annual No. Vol.VIII, No.4-6, Feb. 1973.

9. Benerji, D : "Measurement of Poverty and Under-nutrition", EPW, Vol.XVI, No.39, Sept.26, 1981.

10. Dantwala, M.L. and
    Others : "Search for an Employment, Oriented oriented Growth Strategy": A discussion,EPW,Vol.XXV,No.21,Ma rch26, 1990.

11. Dandekar, V.M : "On Measurement of Poverty", EPW, Vol. XVI, No.30.July 25, 1987.

12. Desai, S.S.M : "Poverty in India - The Magnitude of the Problem", The Economic Times, Vol.VII, No.245, Nov.28, 1980.

13. Gupta, S.P. and
    Dutta, K.L : "Poverty Calculation in the Sixth Plan", EPW, Vol.XIX, No.15, 1984.

14. Hat, N.R : "Poor Are Where They were"? Yojana, Vol.XXVIII, No.9. New Delhi, 1984, May 16-31.

15. Jodha, N.S : "Common Property Resources and Rural Poor in Dry Regions of India", EPW, July 5, 1986.

16. Joshi, P.C : "Perspective on Poverty and Social Change", EPW, Vol.XIV, Nos. 7&8, 1979.

17. Kakwani, N and
    Subba Rao, K : "Rural Poverty and its Alleviation in India", EPW, No.13, March,26, 1990.

18. Krishnaji, N   :   "On Measuring the Incidence of Under
                                nutrition; Anoteon Sukhatme's
                                Procedure", EPW Sept. 12, 1981.

19. Madalgi, S.S   :   Hunger in Rural India : 1960-61 to
                                1964-65", EPW Annual No. January
                                1968.

20. Madalgi, S.S   :   "Poverty in India-A Concept, EPW,
                                February, 20, 1970.

21. Mali, R.L.   :   "Changes in Poverty Levels in
                                Maharasthra", Yojana vol.34 No.5
                                March 16-31, New-Delhi, 1990.

22. Minhas, B.S   :   "Rural Poverty, Land redistribution and
                                Development", Indian Economic
                                Review, Vol.V No.1 April, 1970.

23. Paul, Satya   :   "Unemployment   and
                                Under-employment in Rural India";
                                EPW, July,16,1988.

24. Raj Krishna   :   "Income,   Poverty   and
                                Un-empolyment",
                                EconomicTimes,New-
                                Delhi,May15,1980.

25. Raj Krishna   :   "Small Farmers Development", EPW,
                                May 26, 1979.

26. Hanumantha Rao,   :   "Agricultural Growth and Rural
                                Poverty : Some Lessons from Past
                                Experience, "EPW, Vol.XII.Nos. 33
                                and 34, Special No; August, 1977.

27. Hanumantha Rao,
    G.H. : "Changes in Rural Poverty in India: Implications for Agricultural Growth", Dr.Rajendra Prasad Memorial Lecture, Akhola, December, 29, 1985.

28. Rao, V.K.R.V : "Measurement of Poverty : A note", EPW, Vol.XVI, No.35, August, 29, 1981.

29. Satya Paul : "Some Aspects of House-holds Consumption and Economic Inequalities in Punjab": Phd. Thesis(University of Delhi).

30. Sastry, S.A.R : "Development and Inequality: Across Regional Study", Arthavikas, Gujarat, Vol.16, No.1 (Jan-June) 1980.

31. Sastry, K.V.S &
    Prasad, S.K.(1987) : "Incidence of Poverty and Levels of Development in Rural Andhra Pradesh -A cross section analysis", Annual Conference papers, A.P. Economic Assosiation, University of Hyderabad.

32. Shastry, S.A.R : "A Survey of Literature on Poverty, Income Distribution and Development", Arthvijnana vol.XXII, No.1 March,1980.

33. Sukhatme, P.V : "Incidence of Under-nutrition", Indian Journal of Agricultural Economics, July-September 1977.

34. Vaidyanadhan, A   :   "Some Aspects of Inequalities in living
                               Standards in Rural India", Sankya
                               Series C, Vol.30, 1974.

35. Vyas, V.S   :   "Institutional-Changes, Agricultural
                               Production and Rural Poverty",
                               Commerce,   19th   August,1972.

36. Bhalla, S   :   "Measurement of Poverty: Issuses and
                               Methods", World Bank, 1980 (Mimeo).

37. Choudary,V.R. and
    Sundera Raman   :   "Poverty, Concept and Measurement",
                               Central Statiatical Organisation,
                               New-Delhi (Mimeo).

38. Dantwala, M.L   :   "Poverty and Unemployment in Rural
                               India" Report of the Study conducted
                               with the assistance of International
                               Development Research Centre,
                               Ottawa, Canada, Sept.1973.

39. Gopalan, C, Rama
    Shastry   :   "Nutritive Value of Indian Foods",
                               National Council of Medical Research
                               Hyderabad, India, 1977.

40. Ojha, P.D   ;   "A Configuration of Indian Poverty:
                               Inequality and Levels of Living", RBI
                               Bulletin, January,1970

41. Planning Commission,
    GOI   :   "Seventh Five Year Plan", Government
                               of India. (1980-85).

42. Planning Commission, GOI : "Seventh Five Year Plan" Government of India. (1980-85)

43. Srivastava, S.C. and Others : "People Below Poverty Line: Identification and Strategy for Development", (A diagnostic Case Study of Balla District U.P.), Planning Division, State Planning Institute, Planning Department, Government of U.P. Lucknow, October 1981.

44. Sundaram, K. and Tendulkar, Suresh : "The Poverty Problem"; Seminar 305, Annual, January, 1985.

45. Vinayak Reddy, A. : "Some Technological Changes in Indian Agriculture" Ph.D. Thesis, Department of Economics, Kakatiya University, Warangal, A.P.

INDEX